THE RAPTURE OF THE SAINTS

THE RAPTURE OF THE SAINTS

HERBERT LOCKYER

WHITAKER
HOUSE

Unless otherwise indicated, all Scripture quotations are taken from the King James Version of the Holy Bible. Scripture quotations marked (MOFFATT) are taken from *The Bible: James Moffatt Translation*, © 1922, 1924, 1925, 1926, 1935 by HarperCollins San Francisco; © 1950, 1952, 1953, 1954 by James A. R. Moffatt. Scripture quotations translated by Weymouth are taken from *The New Testament in Modern Speech: An Idiomatic Translation into Everyday English from the Text of "The Resultant Greek Testament"* by R. F. (Richard Francis) Weymouth.

Boldface type in the Scripture quotations indicates the author's emphasis.

THE RAPTURE OF THE SAINTS
Originally published by Pickering & Inglis, London, date unknown, circa 1945.

ISBN: 978-1-62911-740-9
eBook ISBN: 978-1-62911-741-6

© 1979, 2016 by Ardis A. Lockyer

Whitaker House
1030 Hunt Valley Circle
New Kensington, PA 15068
www.whitakerhouse.com

Library of Congress Cataloging-in-Publication Data

Names: Lockyer, Herbert, author.
Title: Rapture of the saints / Herbert Lockyer.
Description: New Kensington, PA : Whitaker House, 2016. | Originally published : London : Pickering & Inglis, circa 1945. | Includes bibliographical references.
Identifiers: LCCN 2016023081 | ISBN 9781629117409 (trade pbk.) Subjects: LCSH: Rapture (Christian eschatology) | Second Advent. Classification: LCC BT887 .L63 2016 | DDC 236/.9—dc23 LC record available at https://lccn.loc.gov/2016023081

No part of this book may be reproduced or transmitted in any form or by any means, electronic or mechanical—including photocopying, recording, or by any information storage and retrieval system—without permission in writing from the publisher. Please direct your inquiries to permissionseditor@whitakerhouse.com.

This book has been printed digitally and produced in a standard specification in order to ensure its continuing availability.

CONTENTS

Introduction 7

1. Old Testament Advent Shadows and
   New Testament Advent Substance 11
2. Conspicuous Aspects of the Advent 23
3. The One Hope of the Advent 33
4. Personal Attitudes Demanded by
   the Advent 45
5. The Sky Symbol of the Advent 51
6. Relationships in the Light of the Advent 57
7. Getting Ready for the Advent 69
8. The Antediluvians and the Advent 79
9. Portents of the Great Tribulation 91

About the Author 105

INTRODUCTION

In this companion volume to *The Sins of Saints*, a word is necessary as to the term *rapture*, used in the title. Although not found in the Bible, the ecstatic experience it represents is fairly common. It is widely accepted as being expressive of the unspeakable joy of being caught up to meet our returning Lord, and the rapturous rejoicing of the saints as they see their Savior in all His beauty and glory. What a moment of amazing wonder it will be when our eyes behold Him!

> Oh, the soul-thrilling rapture when I view His blessed face,
> And the luster of His kindly beaming eye;
> How my full heart will praise Him for the mercy, love, and grace
> That prepared for me a mansion in the sky.[1]

Next to the substitutionary work of Jesus, there is no truth so awe-inspiring and heart-warming as that of His return for those redeemed by His precious blood, as with rapture they look upon His crowned brow, no longer with thorns, but with majesty and glory. In this volume, dealing wholly with the revelation of the second advent of the Lord, I have endeavored to set forth relative aspects of such a blessed event, affecting Jew, Gentile, and the church of God. It is the sincere prayer of the author that the following chapters will prove to be both enlightening and edifying in

---

1. Fanny Crosby, "My Savior First of All," 1894.

the experience of those who study them. The danger is that this sublime truth is deadening when our life and labors are regulated in the light of it. Already the saints are seated in the heavens, and the mission of the Spirit is to make them, as they await the dawning of that glorious morning,

> not less human, but made more divine
> Our lives replete with Heaven's supernal beauty.
> Ever declare that beauty, Lord, is Thine.[2]

If the end of all things is at hand, then our service for the Master will soon cease, our secular and spiritual activities will terminate, our earthly relationships dissolved, our joys and sorrows in this world will be over, our opportunities to witness among the godless concluded. Does not such a glorious appearing of the Son of God call us to prayer for such a grand and glorious event and to desist in trifling, in loitering, and in sinning? If the Lord is at hand, then surely we should be temperate in all things, thinking soberly of ourselves, of others, and of everything around us. Grace must be ours to shun all carelessness or indifference to His commands, and live as those who must give an account of their stewardship or care. It is only when He does come we shall welcome Him with rapture and rejoicing.

> With such a blessed hope in view,
>   We would more holy be!
> More like our coming, glorious Lord
>   Whose face we soon shall see.[3]

John Wesley, founder of Methodism, believed in living in readiness to meet his Lord at any moment. During his remarkable itinerant ministry over Britain, a friend asked him one day, "John, suppose you knew that you were going to die by midnight

---

2. James Mountain, "The Fruit of the Spirit."
3. Stem Publishing, 1843.

tomorrow, how would you spend the rest of your time?" Wesley's answer was characteristic of his devotion to his task:

> I would spend it exactly as I expect to spend it now. I would preach tonight in Gloucester, get up early tomorrow morning and proceed to Tewkesbury, where I would preach in the afternoon. Then I would go to the Martins' house in the evening, as they are expecting me, talk with Mr. Martin, pray with the family, retire, putting myself in the Father's care, go to sleep, and wake up in heaven.

The question for our own heart is "How am I going to live the rest of my time before Jesus comes?" If we knew that within the next twenty-four hours He would return, according to His promise, to take us to the Father's home, are there any circumstances we should immediately change, in the light of such a glorious and blissful event? Or, are we so living in harmony with His will and purpose, that no change of any plan or engagement would be necessary? If, as we await His coming, we are endeavoring to faithfully witness for Him, we shall not be ashamed before Him when He does appear. May He be pleased to use the following chapters for our personal readiness!

1

OLD TESTAMENT ADVENT SHADOWS AND NEW TESTAMENT ADVENT SUBSTANCE

> *Prophecy came not in old time by the will of man: but holy men...spake as they were moved by the Holy Ghost.*
> —2 Peter 1:21

OLD TESTAMENT ADVENT SHADOWS

One of the apostate features of present-day modernism is the disparagement of the Old Testament. Sadly mutilating and dishonorably treating it, the higher critic leaves us with such a remnant of its former self, that one wonders why the Old Testament is not blotted out altogether.

The rejection of the Old Testament, however, carries with it the further rejection of the New Testament, seeing that both sections are two integral parts of one sublime whole. As Dr. A. T. Pierson expresses it in his article, "The Mutual Relations of the Two Testaments":

> These two main divisions resemble the dual structure of the human body, where the two eyes and ears, hands and feet correspond to and complement one another. Not only is there a general, but a special mutual fitness. They need, therefore, to be studied together, side by side; to be

compared even in lesser details, for in nothing are they independent of each other; and the closer the inspection the minuter appears the adaption, and the more intimate the association.[4]

And, further, as Dr. James Orr has pointed out in his masterly work, *The Problem of the Old Testament*, the Old and New Testaments stand or fall together. An organic unity binds them together. "From Genesis to Revelation," says Professor Orr,

> we feel that [the Bible] is in a real sense a unity. It is not a collection of fragments, but has, as we say, an organic character. It has one connected story to tell from beginning to end; we see something growing before our eyes; there is plan, purpose, and progress; the end folds back on the beginning, and, when the whole is finished, we feel that here again, as in the primal creation, God has finished all His works, and behold, they are very good…. The unity of the Bible is not something factitious—*made*. It grows out of the unity of the religion and the history, and points to that as its source.[5]

Dr. A. F. Kirkpatrick, in his *Divine Library of the Old Testament*, has a similar thought: "No other literature is linked into one whole like this; instinct with one spirit and purpose, and, with all its variety of character and origin, moving forward to an unseen yet certain goal."[6]

Such a marvelous unity is only too evident when we come to the study of our Lord's two advents. In fact, as Dr. Pierson reminds

---

4. Arthur Tappen Pierson, "Mutual Relations of the Two Testaments," *Knowing the Scriptures* (New York: Gospel Publishing House, 1910), 52.
5. James Orr, *The Problem of the Old Testament*, vol. 3 (New York: Charles Scribner's Sons, 1907), 32.
6. Alexander Francis Kirkpatrick, *The Divine Library of the Old Testament* (London: Macmillan and Co., 1896), 92.

us, "the only way to read the two Testaments intelligently and adequately is to compare them, to set them side by side; to remember Augustine's great motto, and be prepared to find the Lord Jesus Christ 'latent' in the Old as He is 'patent' in the New."[7] And in his volume on "Many Infallible Proofs," Dr. A. T. Pierson declares that "the prophecies and references to Christ in Old Testament Scripture, which are expressly cited in the New Testament, either as predictions fulfilled in Him, or as previsions applied to Him, number not less than 333." The New is in the Old *concealed*. The Old is in the New *revealed*.

Thus, with the utmost confidence we affirm, as Dr. W. Graham Scroggie does in the admirable treatise on *Christ, the Key to Scripture*, that

> Christ dominates the Old Testament; that He is the Substance of its messages, and the Goal of its hope. If, instead of sucking the dry bones of rationalistic criticism, we were to feed upon the luscious fatness of revealed truth, as centering in and radiating from the Person of Christ, we would be more worthy the name of Christian.[8]

Pages could be written proving how perfectly the Lord Jesus Christ fulfilled all the prophecies regarding His first advent when, in great humility, as the seed of the woman, He made atonement for sin. A thorough study of such an absorbing theme, however, is beyond the scope of this book, but could be pursued elsewhere with success.

Our present purpose is to show that we can learn from the pages of the Old Testament that Jesus is to come again in glorious majesty and power, to "execute judgment and justice and power."

---

7. Pierson, "The Written and Living Word," *Knowing the Scriptures*, 32.
8. W. Graham Scroggie, *Christ, the Key to Scripture* (Philadelphia: The Sunday School Times Company, 1924), 21.

For example, summarizing many of the prophecies of Old Testament writers, we learn that God is to come and judge the earth, that all nations are to serve him, and that Israel is to seek the Lord their God. We also learn that the feet of Jesus are to stand upon the Mount of Olives, that the Holy Spirit is to be poured upon the inhabitants of Jerusalem, and that the dispersed are to be gathered together from the four corners of the earth. In addition, from Old Testament prophecy, we are taught that Christ will be both King and Priest upon His throne, that Jerusalem is to have great prosperity, that all war is to cease, and that eternal joy will be given to the redeemed.

Scriptures to be studied are: Psalm 50:3–6; Psalm 96:11–13; Daniel 7:13–14; Hosea 3:4, 5; Micah 4:7; Zechariah 12:10 and 13:1–6, with Psalm 22:16; Isaiah 11:10–12; Jeremiah 23:5–6; Zechariah 6:12–13, with Psalm 110:4; Isaiah 35:10; Zechariah 2:4–5, 10–11; Ezekiel 37:21–22, 24–26, 27–28; Isaiah 2:2–4; Zechariah 8:7–8, 13–22; Malachi 3:12. If these passages are set down in their order, the student will possess a comprehensive outline of the advent message as contained in the Old Testament.

Of course, it is to be understood that the Old Testament does not furnish us with data regarding the return of Christ for His church, seeing that the church is not a subject of Old Testament revelation. The church, as a very "distinct body of believers, having a distinct mission, and a definite point of beginning, and a definite point of ending," was unknown to Old Testament writers. They saw the two great mountains of Christ's earthly suffering and future glory, but the valleys in between were hid from their gaze. For the fuller revelation of truth, the bud of the Old Testament had to blossom into the flower of the New Testament. The richness and fragrance of such a flower will form the subject of our next meditation.

NEW TESTAMENT ADVENT SUBSTANCE

In Paul's threefold division of the human race, which includes the Jew, the Gentile, and the church of God (see 1 Corinthians 10:32), we discover how to interpret the threefold hope associated with the return of Christ. For example, His advent is:

1. The hope of Israel. The hope of all true Jews is the coming of Christ as their Messiah and deliverer. The Jews still live in the Old Testament, hugging to themselves the predictions regarding the coming of the Messiah. And the hope filling the hearts of many Orthodox Jews today is the vision of the long-promised One. But when they do behold Him, immediate conviction regarding their initial rejection of Christ and unbelief will lay hold of them, for *"they shall look upon me whom they have pierced, and…mourn for him"* (Zechariah 12:10; see also Jeremiah 14:8).

2. The hope of the nations. That the hope of the great Gentile world is Christ's return as king is surely alluded to by the prophet Haggai, who speaks of Him as *"the desire* [or hope, expectation] *of all nations"* (Haggai 2:7). Generally speaking, there is no conscious desire on the part of the nations for Christ. Longings, however, for some masterful man to arrive and rectify the wrongs of the world will only be realized in Christ, when He returns to govern the earth. At present He is "shaking the nations" (see Haggai 2:7), thereby preparing them for His worldwide rule and dominion. The whole creation awaits our Lord's coming, for when He returns to reign, then, and not until then, will universal peace and prosperity be experienced.

3. The hope of the church. It is not death, or even heaven, we are bidden to wait for, but the return of Him who promised to come and receive His church unto Himself. And so she exultantly sings:

Oh hope, all hope surpassing!
Forevermore to be,

> Oh Christ, the Church's Bridegroom,
>   In paradise with Thee.[9]

Dr. David Brown, in a treatise on the second advent written in the 1850s, referred to the personal return of Christ as "the polestar of the church." And it is only as she hitches her wagon to this star that she remains unworldly in life. For the church, the advent is *"that blessed hope"* (Titus 2:13); and it is to this aspect of the hope we are now to address ourselves.

I. THE FACT OF THE ADVENT

There was a time when Christ's first advent was a prophetic truth. (See, for example, Isaiah 7:14; 9:6.) For more than two thousand years such an advent has been an historic fact, as the calendar year proves. The doctrine of His second advent has been a prophetic truth for hundreds of years, being proclaimed by Old and New Testament writers alike. Soon, however, such an advent will be another historic fact. For, as past prophecies relating to Christ's birth and ministry have been fulfilled, so all prophetic Scripture regarding His return are to have as perfect and complete a fulfillment.

Approaching the New Testament advent outline, one discovers a chain of evidence regarding the fact of our Lord's return from its first book to its last. The 260 chapters comprising the New Testament contain more than 300 references to the second coming. More space is given to it than to any other theme, including the death of Christ. The only two New Testament books where no direct evidence can be found are Philemon and the third epistle of John, which of course, were private letters. If, therefore, the truth of our Lord's return occupies such a preeminent place in the Bible, should it not to occupy a corresponding position in our thought and study?

---

9. Horatius Bonar, "The Mountain of Myrrh," 1872.

A full list of advent passages in the twenty-five New Testament books where such a sublime fact is mentioned is unnecessary for present purposes. Let the reader pick up these links in the advent chain: Matthew 24; Mark 13; Luke 21; John 14:1–3; Acts 1:11; Romans 13:11; 1 Corinthians 15:51; 2 Corinthians 5:10; Galatians 5:5; Ephesians 4:30; Philippians 3:20–21; Colossians 3:4; 1 Thessalonians 4:16–17; 2 Thessalonians 1:7–9; 1 Timothy 6:14; 2 Timothy 4:1; Titus 2:13; Hebrews 9:28; James 5:8; 1 Peter 1:3; 2 Peter 1:19; 1 John 2:2–3; 2 John 8; Jude 14–18; Revelation 1:7; 22:20.

A close study of the foregoing passages will reveal how such can be grouped under a threefold classification: the testimony of Christ Himself, the testimony of angels, and the testimony of the Holy Spirit through the church. Further, such a perusal will indicate that each writer emphasizes a different aspect of the advent. For example, Paul is taken up with the rapture of the coming, Peter with the majesty, John with the purity, James with the justice, and Jude with the judgment.

Again, it is imperative to bear in mind that within the advent there are two events; one coming of Christ, but two aspects or parts. Without this distinction, confusion and error will be ours as we seek to bring together what the Scriptures declare regarding Christ's return. First He returns *for* His saints, and then *with* His saints. The first section is associated with the church's translation; the second, with her cooperation. Perhaps the following comparisons will serve to show the distinction between the two.

THE EVENTS OF THE ADVENT

FIRST EVENT	SECOND EVENT
Private (as a king privately visiting close relatives of royal blood)	*Public* (as a king riding in state, and acclaimed everywhere as King)
NT Revelation—e.g., John 14:1–3; Philippians 3:20; 1 Thessalonians 4:15–17.	*OT Prophecy*—e.g., Zechariah 14:5; Colossians 3:4; Jude 14.
Comes to the Air (1 Thessalonians 4:17) *Comes to His Church* *Comes for His Church* *Comes to a Marriage* *Comes as a Bridegroom* *Comes to Gather the Church* (and present it to Himself—a holy and acceptable church)	*Comes to the Mount of Olives* (Zechariah 14:4). *Comes to Israel* *Comes with His Church* *Comes to a Judgment* *Comes as a King* *Comes to Establish His Kingdom* (and with His church reign over the earth in righteousness)
Symbolized by: *Morning Star* *Thief,* coming without warning	Symbolized by: *Rising Sun* *Lightning and Thunder*
Church Caught Away Secretly, into the air: as Enoch before flood; Lot out of Sodom; Elijah.	*Church Openly and Publicly Manifested with Christ,* to assist in His judgment and rule
This event called: *Parousia,* meaning "bodily presence" *Our Gathering unto Him* *The Coming of the Lord*	This event called: *Epiphaneia,* meaning "unveiling of bodily presence." *Our Appearing with Him in Glory* *The Day of the Lord*
This is the hope of the church. *The church listens for sounds.*	*This is the hope of Israel.* *Israel looks for signs.*

It's worth noting that:

1. Between these two events of the second advent there are at least seven prophetic years, known as Daniel's seventieth week. (See Daniel 9:27.) This period forms the burden of the books of Daniel and Revelation.

2. Between us, that is the present church, and the secret coming of our Lord in the air, there is not a single predicted event; there is nothing between.

3. Between us and the second or public part of His coming there are many predicted events awaiting fulfillment; in fact, all that we have in Revelation 4–19.

4. Our twofold responsibility is very clear: (1) In view of the first event, we must live and function as members of His body, so that when we see Him we shall not be ashamed before Him. (2) In view of the second event, we must live as soul-winners, striving to snatch souls out of the awful tribulation awaiting them.

One writer has reminded us that we have a forceful analogy of these two parts of the one advent in the return of France's Charles II after his exile. The two stages of his return were as follows: the first concerned his loyal supporters, who were called across to France *to meet him*. They spent some time there with him, discussing his plan of campaign, and receiving orders and appointments. Then came the second stage, when Charles came back *with them*, and was revealed to the nation as a returning king. He accepted the homage of his subjects and was enthroned. After this came the trial and judgment of the leading rebels. Such a fitting illustration can be easily enlarged upon by the prophetic student.

THE TESTIMONY OF THE AGES

And so leaving this section of our study, it is fitting to observe that the church has never been without witnesses to this most glorious fact of Scripture. All through the ages, the advent message has had its Spirit-inspired heralds. Time fails us to mention them all, but here are a few who have left their imprint upon history: Peter sighed in spirit when he saw certain scoffers arising and denying the promise of the coming; Paul never wrote an epistle without introducing the appeal of the return of his Lord as a sufficient motive for holiness and service. As Massillon has expressed it: "In the days of primitive Christianity it would have been deemed a kind of apostasy not to sigh for the return of the Lord."

The advent was tenaciously held by the early fathers. The late Dr. Guinness declared: "It cannot be denied that for three centuries the church held the doctrine of the pre-millennial coming of Christ. I think I have gone through all the writings of the Fathers for three centuries pretty carefully, and I do not know an exception, unless it be Origen, the only early writer who was often heterodox." The apostolic fathers, then, were unanimous in their declaration of this blessed hope.

The advent has been declared by the outstanding saints of all ages. Time would fail me to tell of all the great, saintly, and scholarly souls who have found the doctrine of the second coming a sufficient incentive to the highest accomplishment. The greatest revivalists of every age, as well as the undaunted missionary pioneers, have all alike been inspired by the preeminent theme of the return of our blessed and kind Lord.

Martin Luther. In the midst of the throes of the Reformation this German monk wrote: "I ardently hope that, amidst these internal dissentions on the earth, Jesus Christ will hasten the day of His Coming."

John Calvin. This acute and learned Genevan reformer also saw that the return of Christ was the church's polestar. "We must hunger after Christ," he said, "till the dawning of that great day when our Lord will manifest the glory of His Kingdom. The whole family of the faithful will keep in view that day."

John Knox. The dauntless soul of this Scottish reformer was also nerved by the *"blessed hope."* In a letter to some English friends he wrote: "Has not the Lord Jesus, in despite of Satan's malice, carried up our flesh into Heaven? And shall He not return? We know that He shall return, and that with expedition."

John Wesley. This great revivalist also believed the same truth regarding the church's hope in the second coming. Commenting upon the closing verses of Revelation, he has this sweet word: "The Spirit of adoption in the bride, in the heart of every true believer, says, with earnest desire and expectation, 'Come, and accomplish all the words of this prophecy.'"

John Milton. The advent of Christ also formed the burden of this wonderful poet's sublime supplication: "Come forth out of Thy royal chambers, O Prince of all the kings of the earth; put on the visible robes of Thy imperial majesty: take up that unlimited scepter which Thy Almighty Father hath bequeathed Thee. For now the voice of Thy bride calls Thee, and all creatures sigh to be renewed."

Samuel Rutherford. Christ's second coming was also the ardent longing of the seraphic Rutherford: "Oh, that Christ would remove the covering, draw aside the curtain of time, and come down! Oh, that the shadows of the night were gone!"

Such testimonies to the fact of the second coming could be multiplied a thousand times over. Every generation has produced those who, with faces uplifted toward the veil within which the Lord of Glory patiently waits, and with hearts all aglow with a personal love for Him, have lived, and loved, and labored in the light of His glorious appearing. It has been their "polestar." Such a fact, however, is openly discredited today. Modernism speaks of a golden age, but will not have the New Testament revelation of those processes producing such. Our obligation is clear. Knowing and believing the fact of Christ's return, we must declare it, trusting the Holy Spirit to bless and use our witness.

2

CONSPICUOUS ASPECTS OF THE ADVENT

This same Jesus, which is taken up from you into heaven, shall so come in like manner as ye have seen him go into heaven.
—Acts 1:11

This chapter is a study of the concluding chapter on "The Lord's Coming" in The Mackintosh Treasury. *This book is a marvelous coverage of this heart-warming theme, published by Loizeaux Brothers, Inc., Neptune, New Jersey. It will greatly assist the reader in grasping the details associated with the succeeding events in our Lord's second advent.* Of the many branches of this great and glorious event, C-H-M, as Charles Henry Mackintosh, renowned Bible expositor of the eighteenth century was known, says that "the theme is intensely interesting, deeply practical, and abundantly fruitful. Moreover, it is very suggestive and often is an extensive field of vision for the spiritual mind to range through with an interest that never flags, because the subject is inexhaustible."[10]

THE TIME OF THE ADVENT

As the doctrine of the second coming has been spurned by many, because of the unscriptural and unwise treatment meted

---

10. Charles Henry Mackintosh, *Things New and Old*, vol. 15 (London: G. Morrish, 1872), 182.

out to it by some preachers and teachers, especially regarding the *fixing of dates*, we deem it necessary to declare that the time of our Lord's return is, from this side of heaven, unknown. The day has been marked on God's calendar, and therefore, He alone is cognizant of the precise moment when His beloved Son will rend the heavens and come down. *"It is not for you to **know the times** or the seasons, which the Father hath put in his own power"* (Acts 1:7).

Turning to the New Testament, we discover three classes of passages connected with the "time" aspect of this soul-absorbing theme, which if kept in mind, will save us from extravagance in fixing definite dates for the appearing of our blessed Lord. Pastor Russell declared that Christ came in 1874. Later on, this man, who believed that the millennium had dawned, put the date forward several years. Alas, some more orthodox and saintly than Pastor Russell have erred in this date-fixing despite the: (a) passages suggesting uncertainty (Matthew 24:26, 42, 44; 1 Thessalonians 5:1–2); (b) passages suggesting speed (Matthew 24:39; Revelation 3:11); and (c) passages suggesting delay (Matthew 24:48; 25:19; 2 Peter 3:4).

With such Scripture before him, no man has any warrant for date-fixing. To predict dates is to falsify our position, and to contradict the Word of God. The *fact* of His coming is *certain*, and this is sufficient for the comfort of our hearts; the *time* of His coming is *uncertain*, and that is sufficient for the consecration of our lives. As one has reminded us, there is enough certainty to feed the lamp of our faith, and enough uncertainty to make us very careful in case, when the Bridegroom comes, our lamps will have gone out. The uncertain hour of Christ's certain appearing calls for constant readiness. He may return at any moment, and therefore we must live moment by moment in the attitude of preparedness, so that His coming will not overtake us unawares, causing us to be ashamed. Said an old Scottish peasant woman: "I dinna ken when He is coming, but I'll be gey glad to see Him when He comes." And if we are to be "gey glad to see Him when He comes," our whole life must be guided by the light streaming from such a "polestar."

> Ready to seek, ready to warn,
> Ready o'er souls to yearn;
> Ready in life, ready in death,
> Ready for His Return.[11]

THE MANNER OF THE ADVENT

When our glorious Lord went back to heaven, leaving His awe-stricken disciples gazing up at the cloud which, as a chariot, bore Him back to glory, the angelic assurance received was that He would return the same way, that *"this same Jesus...shall so come in like manner as ye have seen him go..."* (Acts 1:11).

And the phrase *"in like manner"* cannot mean anything else than "in manner like to." Christ's return then is to correspond, and take place in the same way, to His ascension. Well, how did He go?

1. HIS GOING WAS CERTAIN

The disciples saw Jesus go, and the angels saw Him arrive. The ascension of Christ was not a vision, but a fact. And, just as certainly as He went away, so does He declare the certainty of His return, stating, *"I will come again..."* (John 14:3).

2. HIS GOING WAS IN THE PRESENCE OF BELIEVERS

The last time the world saw the Savior was at His rejection. *"Ye shall not see me henceforth..."* (Matthew 23:39). The last vision the godless had of Christ was at the cross, where they dealt with Him. Their next vision of Him will be at the judgment, when He will deal with them.

---

11. From the Christian Worker's Motto.

The last time the disciples saw Jesus was at the Mount of Olives, as He ascended up on high. The next viewpoint from earth will be at His return, when all His saints will gaze upon Him as the descending Bridegroom. Our eyes will not be hidden then. Scales, however, will be upon the eyes of the godless at His coming.

3. HIS GOING WAS SECRET

The ascension was only known to, and witnessed by, a few men of Galilee. The rest of the world was ignorant of such a sublime fact. And His return, said the angelic messengers, is to be in like manner. Apart from His own, none will be aware of such a great event and advent. Secular historians recorded the story of Christ's life and death in about four lines; and if that is all the impression His first coming made upon the world of that day, it is certain that His second coming will not cause much stir in our godless age. Here and there, a few so-called narrow-minded Christians will be missed, but the whole matter will be a nine-day wonder. Quickly the world will resume its heedless course, captivated by the delusion of the superman, until the blow falls in such a way as to cause universal despair and death.

4. HIS GOING WAS SUDDEN

We talk about sudden death when one disappears from our midst in a moment of time. Well, the ascension of Christ was a sudden departure, for one moment He was talking to His disciples, and the next He was in heaven. And His advent is to be as sudden. Paul tells us that He is coming in *"the twinkling of an eye"* (1 Corinthians 15:52). And such a striking figure implies speed; for the winking of the eye is the quickest movement of the human body.

5. HIS GOING WAS PERSONAL

The disciples saw the actual Christ ascend, otherwise the language of the angels about *"this same Jesus"* returning has no meaning. What was the manner of His going? Actual, visible, tangible, corporeal; so shall He come! Would that expositors could lay hold of this truth, and not make the promise of Jesus, in John 14:3, to mean Pentecost, the destruction of Jerusalem, death, providential experiences. When He said, *"I will come again,"* He meant what He said. The New Testament advent word is *parousia*, meaning the arrival, or coming, of a person. Yes, we look for Him, and not for another; *"this **same** Jesus"*—*"the Lord himself"*—*"I **come** quickly"* (Acts 1:11; 1 Thessalonians 4:16; Revelation 22:20).

6. HIS GOING WAS IN CLOUDS

Christ was taken or carried up in clouds. The clouds were His chariots; and such are associated with His coming. (See Matthew 24:30; Jude 14; Revelation 1:7, etc.) Paul, however, has a sweet word about the clouds, for he tells us we are to be *"caught up together… in the clouds"* (1 Thessalonians 4:17). And, as Dr. Middleton suggests, the clouds here are not ethereal, but clouds of believers. (See Hebrews 12:1.) Caught up in clouds! A cloud from America, a cloud from Britain! Will you be among the cloud going up from your own city or town?

THE STAGES OF THE ADVENT

There are those who would have us believe that we have no authority for defining the various stages constituting the miracle of the Lord's coming. But while liberty of thought can be allowed over details, surely *"rightly dividing the word of truth"* (2 Timothy 2:15) means that we can discover from God's Word what the Holy Spirit has so clearly defined regarding those things that must happen at Christ's return. What, then, is the broad outline of the advent experiences?

1. THE SOUNDS OF DESCENSION

The apostle Paul reminds us that the Lord is to descend with "*a shout…voice…trump*" (1 Thessalonians 4:16). These military words are not exactly equivalent. Trumpets were used in gathering the hosts of Israel. (See Numbers 10:4.) At the first and second blasts the people were gathered, and at the third trump they had to march and follow their leader.

The dead are to rise. Responding to the victor's shout, the shout of command, the graves yield up their precious dust.

The living are changed. At the sound of the archangel's commanding voice, the bodies of saints alive at Christ's return will be immediately transformed. The accents of this majestic voice will not be detected by a deaf world.

The "raised" and the "changed" are caught up together. With the trump of God, the church jubilant and the church militant become the church glorified, which rises out of a world of sin to meet her glorious Lord. The last trump issues the call to ascend, and then rejoice with our Captain in His final conquests. (See Psalm 50:4, 5.)

2. THE RESURRECTION OF THE DEAD

It is very clear, from Paul's writing, that "the sky, not the grave, is our goal."[12] The dead are to be raised. (See 1 Thessalonians 4:16; 1 Corinthians 15:52.) Notice must be taken of the fact, however, that only a particular class of the dead participates in this advent resurrection. Paul terms them *"the dead in Christ."* This is a resurrection "out from among" the dead. The rest of the dead are left in their graves until the resurrection and judgment of Revelation 20:5 takes place.

---

12. Horatio G. Spafford, "It Is Well with My Soul," 1873.

The spirits of our loved ones who died in Christ have been with Him ever since their departure, and at Christ's advent are to return with their Lord. (See Philippians 1:23; 1 Thessalonians 4:14.) The miracle our Lord performs is the gathering of the dust, sleeping in the grave, and the transforming of such into a body like unto His own glorious body. (See Philippians 3:21.) This is the phase of redemption awaiting fulfillment. (See Romans 8:23; Ephesians 4:30.)

3. THE TRANSFORMATION OF THE LIVING

If we have bodies subject to sickness and disease, and riddled with pain, here is a blessed thought to inspire us anew: we shall be changed! (See 1 Thessalonians 4:15, 17; 1 Corinthians 15:51, 52; Philippians 3:21.) And these soul-stirring passages imply that at Christ's coming all the living saints are to receive spiritual, sinless, ethereal bodies like unto our Lord's. When we see Him we shall be *like* Him! (See 1 John 3:2.) We are told that our present bodies change every seven years. Well, their final change is coming! And as the body is the source of sin and the seat of weakness, what a welcome change awaits it!

4. THE SIMULTANEOUS TRANSLATION OF BOTH

All the raised and all the changed are to be *"caught up **together**,"* says the apostle (1 Thessalonians 4:17). The partial rapture theory, then, is erroneous. Not a hoof will be left behind! This event, or stage, concerns *"they that are Christ's"* (1 Corinthians 15:23). The phrase *"caught up"* is a descriptive one. It means to snatch away by force, as a wild beast seizes and carries off its prey. It also implies to be snatched away out of danger, as a child is sometimes delivered from the cruel death a passing vehicle would cause. And so the saints are to be snatched away before the terrible tribulation overtakes a godless world. Lot being snatched out of Sodom is a striking illustration of this point. The departure of the church will be the signal for the outpouring of sorrow upon the earth.

This sweet fellowship word *"together"* is worth lingering over for a moment. It carries with it the thought of reunion. Many have empty chairs and emptier hearts. Death has separated friend from friend. At Christ's return, however, we shall be *"together"* once again. Together forever.

> Some from earth, from glory some,
> Severed only till He come.[13]

There is also the idea of unity in Paul's word. Earnest-minded leaders are working for the union of all branches of the church down here. They are out to produce a "togetherness," impressive in its strength. Well, the advent alone can realize this ideal! Now we are sadly divided by our theological differences and denominational barriers. After the advent, we shall be *"together."* May the Lord hasten such a blissful union!

5. THE GLORIOUS MEETING IN THE AIR

For the purposes of commerce, travel, and war, all nations are concentrating upon the air. Aviation predominates in every country. The motto of our Air Force is significant: *"Per Ardu ad Astra,"* that is, "Through difficulties to the stars."

And is it not somewhat strange that while the wise of the earth are endeavoring to explore the secrets of the air, the saints are thinking about their rapture in the air? We are *"to meet the Lord in the air"* (1 Thessalonians 4:17). Airplanes, as a mechanical invention, have no personal attraction in the air. Nothing draws them up. They rise by their own power or volition. Our ascent will be different. We are to be caught or drawn up to our halfway house. As filings leaping to the magnet, Christ will draw all saints up to

---

13. Edward H. Bickersteth, "Till He Come," 1861.

Himself. Yes, and ours will be the greatest flight of all, for we shall stay up! Drawn up to meet the Lord! Oh, what rapture will be ours as we gaze upon His face!

6. THE "JUDGMENT SEAT OF CHRIST"

After translation there comes rectification. Particulars of this judgment, or "Bema,"[14] can be found in 1 Corinthians 3:12–15; 2 Corinthians 5:10; Romans 14:10; Revelation 22:12, and so forth. As we hope to deal with this stage of our glorification in a separate article, suffice it to say that this private judgment is necessary in three particulars:

1. To adjust the tangles, differences, and estrangements between believers.

2. To test, or judge, the real nature of our earthly service.

3. To determine our rank or position in the coming kingdom.

And it is but fitting that the rectification of the Bema, or "judgment seat," should precede the jubilation of the marriage feast. For we cannot enter into the joy of the blissful union associated with marriage unless there is perfect love and perfect understanding. The Bema will put us right with one another and with the Lord; and then, with nothing between, we can go forward.

7. THE MARRIAGE SUPPER OF THE LAMB

Doubtless the language of Revelation 19:7–9 is figurative, depicting, as it does, the culmination of the bliss of the glorified. After the judgment there comes the joy! Mutual love and harmony prevails, once the Bema has done its testing work. What a blessed prospect is ours! May we live and labor in the light of it! With faces uplifted toward the veil, within which the Lord of glory patiently

---

14. "Bema Seat" is a term taken from the name of the judge's seat in athletic competitions in ancient Greece and used to describe God's apportioning of reward to believers in the end times.

waits, and with hearts all aglow with a deep and ever-deepening love for Him, let us echo the prayer of Richard Baxter: "Hasten, O my Savior, the time of thy return; send forth thine angels, and let that dreadful, joyful trumpet sound.... Thy desolate bride saith *come*...the whole creation saith *come*...even so, come, Lord Jesus."[15]

Taking leave of our meditation upon this "Advent Outline," we would summarize the teaching of the New Testament thus:

Christ taught His disciples to expect His return.

The apostles taught their converts the same truth.

The whole life and work of the New Testament church has His coming in view.

The grace of hope rests upon our Lord's advent.

Redemption is not complete until Jesus comes.

The coming of Christ will realize God's purpose in creation.

The blessed hope is the Christian's most inspiring motive in life and service.

---

15. Richard Baxter, *The Saints' Everlasting Rest* (New York: Joshua Soule and Thomas Mason, 1817), 307.

3

THE ONE HOPE OF THE ADVENT

One hope of your calling....
—Ephesians 4:4

The believer has only one hope, namely, that blessed hope of which the apostle Paul wrote (see Titus 2:13); and which he designates as the *one* hope of our calling (see Ephesians 4:4). Very often we come across those who, when asked if they are saved, reply, "I hope so." Such an answer, of course, is wrong, seeing that salvation is a present possession, while hope is the expectation of something future.

The elements of hope are desire, expectation, and patience. The word itself implies the idea of cherishing something beneficial with the expectation of obtaining it, or to desire with expectation or with the belief in the profit of obtaining. Hope is not desire merely, for we may desire what we do not expect. For example, a man desires great wealth, but never expects to possess it. Hope is not expectation only, for a person may expect what he does not desire. A person may be expecting to die from some dread disease, and yet not desire death. Hope is desire and expectation combined and exercised with that patience or endurance which can wait for the full realization.

As *"hope"* is one of the dominant words of the New Testament, let us classify the references where this advent word is to be found.

I. THE CONTENT OF OUR HOPE

The *"hope"* brought before us in the gospel is not elusive, vain, mythical, or visionary, but real, tangible, substantial. Thomas Chalmers declared that "the grand essentials of life are something to do, something to love, something to hope for." Well, the believer has something to do—work for Christ; something to love—the Word of Christ; and something to hope for—the return of Christ. Among the contents of our hope, we trace the following:

1. Christ: *"Lord Jesus Christ, which is our hope"* (1 Timothy 1:1).

So our hope is not merely an event or advent, but the coming of a Person. Let us not get lost in a maze of details concerning prophecy. Someone is coming! Let us keep our eyes on the One soon to appear.

2. Salvation: *"putting on…for an helmet, the hope of salvation"* (1 Thessalonians 5:8).

Paul was very careful about his phraseology. Our helmet is not hope *for* salvation, but *"the hope of salvation."* A helmet preserves from defeat; and the advent helmet serves to deliver us from all spiritual defeat.

3. Grace: *"hope to the end for the grace that is to be brought unto you at the revelation of Jesus Christ"* (1 Peter 1:13).

The final work of grace is to bring us to Him who came as the personification of the grace of God. Our translation, then, like our salvation, is all of grace. Our rapture does not depend upon works.

4. Resurrection: *"the hope and resurrection of the dead…"* (Acts 23:6; 24:15).

Death may blast many earthly hopes, but here is a hope the grave can never wither. The sky, not the grave, is our goal! As the farmer sows his seed in the hope of gathering fruit, so our gathering unto Him is the hope of resurrection. And what a harvest will be His at His coming!

5. Eternal Life: *"In hope of eternal life…"* (Titus 1:2).

Eternal life, then, is wrapped up in this blessed hope. And this hope promised before the world began is now ours by faith. The full realization of this life, however, is future. We are heirs according to the hope of eternal life. (See Titus 3:7.) Heirs! We are to come into our full possessions when Christ returns.

6. Righteousness: *"For we through the Spirit wait for the hope of righteousness by faith"* (Galatians 5:5).

Two truths emerge from this aspect of hope. First, we are enabled by the Holy Spirit to wait and hope. Second, our hope is one of righteousness. Such a hope can make us righteous in character. It will also bring us to the completion of our righteousness in Him. Now we have a righteous standing. When Jesus comes, we shall enter into our eternally righteous state.

7. Glory: *"the hope of glory"* (Colossians 1:27).

The indwelling Christ, as the hope of glory, is spoken of as *"the riches of the glory of this mystery"* (verse 27) of the gospel. As believers, we know that the hope we are considering will be realized, for the Christ within is the pledge of its realization. The spiritual Christ is to take us up to the personal Christ. What a glorious hope! And as all believers are indwelt by Christ, all are to share in the rapture.

8. Calling: *"The hope of his calling…his inheritance in the saints"* (Ephesians 1:18).

Our inheritance, His inheritance. (See Ephesians 1:14, 18.) His hope, when He called us, was to have us altogether with Himself. Our hope, now that we are His, is the joy of being near to His side forever.

II. THE CHARACTER OF OUR HOPE

Examining further "hope" passages, faith delights to feast upon the manifold character of the "blessed hope," which the old divines were fond of calling "the polestar of the church."

1. Personal: *"My earnest expectation and my hope…"* (Philippians 1:20; see also Romans 15:4; 2 Corinthians 3:12; 1 John 3:3).

Alas, the coming of the Lord is not the hope of every believer. Some are ignorant of such a truth. Others scorn it and disbelieve it. And there are yet others, who, although they believe it, are not ready to meet the Lord. May we each have a personal faith in the personal return of the Lord!

2. Indwelling: *"the hope that is in **you**…"* (1 Peter 3:15).

The believer possesses an indwelling Lord, an indwelling Spirit, an indwelling Hope. And such a Hope is *in* the saint, seeing that Christ is *within*. Yes, and being within, this hope can influence the whole inner life.

3. Living: *"hath begotten us again unto a lively hope…"* (1 Peter 1:3).

The second advent is a living hope, seeing that it is centered on a living Lord. And this hope creates, sustains life. There can be no true, abundant life where the coming of Christ is neglected.

4. Good: *"everlasting consolation and good hope through grace"* (2 Thessalonians 2:16).

One meaning of "good" is *beautiful*. Thus the return of the King whom we are to see in His beauty can be likened unto a beautiful hope. Acceptance of this fundamental truth beautifies character. The next verse speaks about being *"stablish*[ed]*…in every good word and work"* (verse 17) and faith in Christ's return is not impractical, it inspires beautiful words and beautiful works.

5. Blessed: *"Looking for that blessed hope…"* (Titus 2:13).

Blessed, we are told, means "happy." Think of the happiness the second coming will occasion to the Lord Himself, to ourselves, to loved ones gone before. Christ's advent is likewise a blessed hope, seeing that it is to usher the believer into the climax of all blessings.

6. Joyous: *"Rejoicing in hope"* (Romans 12:12).

Knowing that Christ is on the wing enables us to rejoice even amid tribulation. The sufferings of this present time are real, even to the child of God. But he sings although he sighs, knowing that his redemption draws near.

7. Emboldening: *"And hope maketh not ashamed…"* (Romans 5:5).

Such a hope is not false or elusive. Christ is coming according to His promise. He will not give us shamedness of face through failing to appear. And, further, having this hope we can laugh at the sneers of those who spurn our witness for Christ.

8. Sure and steadfast: *"Which hope we have as an anchor of the soul, both sure and stedfast…"* (Hebrews 6:19).

An anchor grips an unseen foundation, and our anchor is within the veil. An anchor also keeps a ship from drifting, and the blessed hope likewise prevents a Christian or a church from drifting very far from God and His Word.

9. Better: *"a better hope…by the which we draw nigh unto God"* (Hebrews 7:19).

The world is hoping to have a better time, industrially, socially, and economically. The world, however, is without any better hope. It hopes against hope. God's Word declares that those in the world who love its ways are destitute of hope, and have not a solitary hope. (See also Ephesians 2:12; 1 Thessalonians 4:13.)

There are those who hope to get to heaven and hope God will not be too hard on them, but such do not constitute the *"better hope."* The nature of our hope consists of the knowledge that

Christ, by His death, made possible our salvation, and that one day He is coming for our deliverance from a sinful nature and a sinning world.

III. THE CLAIMS OF OUR HOPE

Hope cannot be possessed in any detached way. It demands much of those who hold it and who are held by it. Hope has been called the salt and sinew of life. Well, the blessed hope is certainly the salt and sinew of our Christian life. Let us examine some of its claims.

1. Profession: *"Let us hold fast the profession of our faith without wavering…"* (Hebrews 10:23).

Others may deny Christ's coming, but our obligation is to declare it, and do so unflinchingly. We must hold it fast, and it must hold us fast. May God deliver the pulpits of the land from sinful silence concerning our Lord's return.

2. Boasting: *"hold fast the confidence and the rejoicing of the hope firm unto the end"* (Hebrews 3:6).

Amid the futile schemes of men for the alleviation of the world's need is it not something to be bold and boast about knowledge that Jesus is on the way to clear up the mess of earth for which Satan and man are responsible? We glory in the coming, seeing that it is the only solution for the world's chaotic condition.

3. Explanation: *"be ready always to give an answer to every man that asketh you a reason of the hope that is in you…"* (1 Peter 3:15).

Everywhere there are inquiring hearts. Because of bias, prejudice, ignorance, or error, many do not know what the Scripture has to say about the return of Christ in the air for His own. Let us, therefore, clearly grasp the broad and general outline of such a truth so that we may be always ready to explain our hope to those without hope.

4. Purity: *"And every man that hath this hope in him purifieth himself, even as he [Christ] is pure"* (1 John 3:3).

Like, we say, begets like. Believers, therefore, can never be unclean, or worldly in thought or life if they constantly live under the sanctifying influence of the truth concerning our Lord's imminent return. The coming of Him, who is pure and holy, makes for the purification of every part of life.

5. Endurance: *"patience of hope…"* (1 Thessalonians 1:3).

Christ's return is the stay in all our endurance, the strength in all our enterprise, the solace in all our sorrow, and the spur to all our effort. Without such a hope we would droop beneath our burdens.

> Oh blessed hope with this elate,
> Let not our hearts be desolate,
> But strong in faith, in patience wait
>   Until He come![16]

6. Assurance: *"the full assurance of hope unto the end…"* (Hebrews 6:11).

Many Christians lack the assurance of the coming as well as the assurance of salvation. But with our Lord's explicit promise before us, we should have no doubt about His return. *"I will come again, and receive you unto myself"* (John 14:3). And He was not a man that He should lie.

> He tells me He is coming,
> And that's quite enough for me.[17]

7. Abundance: *"abound in hope…"* (Romans 15:13).

To abound means to have more than enough. Are we so taken up with the second advent as to feel that the provisions of the future

---
16. George Rawson, "By Christ Redeemed, in Christ Restored," 1857.
17. H. Green, "He Is Not a Disappointment!"

are more than enough? Samuel Rutherford often spoke of his Lord as "the ever-running-over Lord Jesus." And, in like manner, our hope is an "ever-running-over" one. Oh, that our whole being might be captivated by the glories yet to be revealed!

IV. THE CONDITIONS OF OUR HOPE

Turning to further passages where "hope" is to be found, the following classification of its conditions may prove to be helpful.

1. God is its author: *"the God of hope…"* (Romans 15:13).

Alas, many of His hopes concerning man are blasted, but this hope is certain of realization. In spite of all antagonistic forces, His own will ultimately be with Him and share His glory. This is the hope of His calling. (See Ephesians 1:18.) Notice the threefold aspect of the blessed hope as related to the Lord:

A. He is the object of it: *"in whom we trust* [set our hope]" (2 Corinthians 1:10); *"and have hope toward God…"* (Acts 24:15); *"your…hope might be in God"* (1 Peter 1:21).

B. He is the foundation of it: *"we trust in the living God…"* (1 Timothy 4:10; see also 1 Timothy 5:5; 6:17; 1 Peter 1:13; 3:5).

C. He is the sphere of it: *"hope in Christ…"* (1 Corinthians 15:19). The key words, then, are "toward," "upon," and "within."

2. The gospel is its revelation: *"the hope of the gospel…"* (Colossians 1:23).

Apart from the Scriptures, we have no light regarding the sublime truth of Christ's return. And it was to the apostle Paul that the privilege of bearing the full revelation of such a fundamental theme was granted.

3. The Scriptures are its warrant: *"we through…the scriptures might have hope"* (Romans 15:4).

The Bible is an advent book. Every book, for example, in the New Testament, with the exception of Philemon and 3 John, deals with Christ's coming from a different angle. In fact, more space is devoted to this doctrine than to any other.

4. Christ is its sustenance: *"Christ in you, the hope of glory"* (Colossians 1:27).

His presence within the heart feeds this hope. His indwelling is a guarantee of its fulfillment.

5. The Holy Spirit is its supply: *"abound in hope, through the... Holy Ghost"* (Romans 15:13).

It is He who helps us to understand this truth. It is His function to unfold the things to come. And it is He who groans within us for the coming of the Bridegroom.

6. Heaven is its incentive: *"For the hope which is laid up for you in heaven..."* (Colossians 1:5; see also Hebrews 11:16).

At His coming, Christ is to usher us into His own immediate presence. Then will His express wish of John 17:24 be realized: *"Father, I will that they also...be with me where I am; that they may behold my glory...."*

7. Faith is its basis: *"Now faith is the substance of things hoped for..."* (Hebrews 11:1; see also 1 Corinthians 13:13).

In this hope we were saved. We are not saved by hope, but by faith. We were saved, however, with reference to hope, namely the blessed hope revealed in the gospel. (See Romans 8:23-24.)

FAITH	HOPE
Faith looks backward.	Hope looks onward and upward.
Faith is concerned with the Person who promises.	Hope with the thing promised.
Faith accepts.	Hope expects.
Faith appropriates.	Hope anticipates.
Faith believes and takes.	Hope desires and waits.
Faith comes by hearing.	Hope comes by experience.
Faith is the root.	Hope is the fruit.

Let us all, then, crave:

Faith's patience imperturbable in Thee,
Hope's patience till the long-drawn shadows flee.[18]

A gifted writer draws attention to the fact that when the king was heralded in Zechariah 9:9, the appeal went out to the enslaved: *"Turn you to the strong hold, ye prisoners of hope"* (Zechariah 9:12). In the age-old prison of Field Castle on one of the Channel Islands, the place of incarceration for political prisoners was called "Hope Cell." Those sent there by the rulers of England were confined at the king's pleasure. Then, what hope could be attached to the sorry plight? Just this, that at the death of the king such prisoners obtained their release. The believers' King has died. The regal title was inscribed about His cross. He entered the strong man's palace and opened the gates to eternal freedom, and now:

My chains are snapped,
The bonds of sin are broken
    And I am free,

---

18. Christina Rossetti, "Lord, It Is Good for Us to Be Here," *Verses* (New York: E. and J. B. Young & Co., 1893), 117.

Oh, let the triumphs of His grace be spoken
   Who died for me.[19]

But, delivered, we are still prisoners of hope. Confined in "Hope Cell," we sigh for emancipation from the trammeling influences of the flesh and the world. And, praise God, our crucified, risen, glorified King is coming for our release. Before long He will turn aside from the ivory palaces and with joy we shall respond to His call of *"rise up, my love, my fair one, and come away"* (Song of Solomon 2:10).

---

19. Margaret L. Carson, "My Chains are Snapped."

4

PERSONAL ATTITUDES DEMANDED BY THE ADVENT

*Blessed is that servant,
whom his lord when he cometh shall find so doing.*
—Matthew 24:46

Because every truth of God is a deadening truth unless it becomes a functional truth in our lives, it is beneficial to us to examine the attitude we ought to maintain toward the sublime message of our Lord's return. The Master Himself hinted at the saint's attitude in view of His appearing: *"Blessed is that servant, whom his lord when he cometh shall find so doing"* (Matthew 24:46). Two thoughts emerge from this declaration:

The announcement: *"His lord when he cometh."* The great theme of our Lord's coming is inexhaustible. Like the prism, it is many-colored. And, as the blessed or blissful hope, it transforms us into its very nature the more we meditate upon it.

The attitude: *"Shall find so doing."* The New Testament suggests several aspects of the saints' attitude regarding the coming of our Lord. We are, for example, exhorted to:

PRAY FOR HIS COMING

In the so-called Lord's Prayer we have the petition: *"Thy kingdom come,"* or *"Thy reign begin"* (Matthew 6:10). John prayed a similar prayer when he uttered the cry, *"Even so, come, Lord Jesus"* (Revelation 22:20). And when we think of the state of the world and of society, of the great upheaval of our day, what other prayer can we pray?

> What a hope for the world's regeneration the thought should stir in me! This is the Gospel for north and south alike. This is the salvation which is without boundary and shore. This is the potency, and this is the love, that are the same under every sky. Ay, and when peoples and nations and kindred and tongues accept His grace, they are coming back to their true home.[20]

And yet, with multitudes in darkness, and loved ones still unsaved, can we utter such a prayer, knowing that the speedy return of Christ would mean the eternal banishment of some who are dearest from the presence of the Lord? Yes, we can pray for His coming, for true intercession prevails. Pleading for the Lord to return, we redouble our efforts to rescue the perishing. The service that counts in a world of sin is ever the service inspired by *"that blessed hope"* (Titus 2:13).

BELIEVE HIS COMING

Such was the thoroughness of the apostle Paul that, while at Thessalonica for a month's mission, he instructed the converts in all the fundamental doctrines of the New Testament. This is why, in writing to them at a later period, he says: *"we believe…the Lord himself shall descend…"* (1 Thessalonians 4:14, 16). And if the Redeemer's coming is "the polestar of the church," then the sooner the church returns to such a polestar, and guides its course by the light of it, the quicker will the church realize its divine function in the world. The tragedy, however, of our modern day is that the His coming is doubted, criticized, ridiculed, and neglected. Sad to

---

20. Alexander Smellie, *In the Secret Place* (London: Andrew Melrose, 1808), 32.

relate, the coming is not generally believed in among church-going people. There is a lamentable ignorance regarding the simple outline of prophetical truth, even among many Christians.

WAIT FOR HIS COMING

Paul, the advent apostle, has a striking word about the advent attitude in his second epistle to the Thessalonians: *"the Lord direct your hearts…into the patient waiting for Christ"* (3:5). The word *"waiting"* implies a bearing up under, or patient endurance of, evil and trial and sorrow. No matter how heavy our load we must bear up, for Jesus, the Load-lifter, is at hand!

The phrase, however, has a double significance. Not only must the saint patiently wait for Christ, but as the margin suggests, he must exhibit the very patience of Christ. Weymouth translates it: *"May the Lord guide [you]…into the patience of Christ,"* or *"Christ's patience,"* as Moffatt puts it. In yonder glory, Jesus is patiently waiting, and has been for more than two millennia, to overthrow the wrong, and diadem the right. Patiently, He sits waiting to glorify His own, and to deliver a groaning creation. And we are called to manifest His patience.

LOVE HIS COMING

Are we aware of the fact that a special crown is to be bestowed upon the saints who have *"loved and longed for his appearance"*? (2 Timothy 4:8 MOFFATT). Loved and longed for! It is an expressive translation. Weymouth translates it: *"Love the thought of His Appearing."* Not only the appearing, but the very thought of it! What an attitude! Is it ours? Do we allow the coming to control our thoughts, words, and actions?

Our hearts experience a peculiar thrill as the object of love appears. Do our innermost beings rise in adoring praise at the thought of Christ's return? Oh, to recover the thrill as we study such a theme! May ours be the crown awaiting all those who love and long for His appearing!

PREACH HIS COMING

Writing to a young evangelist, Paul offered a little advice, so sadly neglected in these days of speculation and theories: *"Preach the word"* (2 Timothy 4:2). And part of this Word is in the first verse: *"The Lord Jesus Christ, who shall judge the quick and the dead at his appearing and his kingdom."* But there is a sinful silence in our pulpits regarding this essential part of the Word. Why, if all the ministers of our land preached for a month on the Lord's second coming, revival would sweep through the country like a torrent! For this we are grateful, namely, that the advent witness is growing. There was never a time when such interest was manifested in prophecy as at the present moment. Wherever this phrase of the Word is preached, there is never lacking an eager audience.

LOOK FOR HIS COMING

We here strike an oft-repeated advent attitude. *Watch* is a word constantly falling from the lips of our Lord. Paul tells us to "look" for that blessed hope (see Titus 2:13). This word "look" has a twofold meaning; first, to look away from one thing so as to see another. This thought is resident in the phrase *"looking unto Jesus"* (Hebrews 12:2); that is, look away from all else to Him. So many have their eyes glued on this world that they fail to see another. Let us turn our eyes upon Jesus and His appearing, then we shall discover how strangely dim the things of earth really are.

In the second place, the word *look* means to bend forward, or to look intently. *"Why look ye so earnestly on us?"* (Acts 3:12). A royal personage is about to visit a city, and the roads are thronged with eager crowds waiting to catch a glimpse of him. At last he comes, and necks are strained forward to see what he is like, as he passes by. Such is the attitude suggested by Paul's word.

DESPISE HIS COMING

Peter reminds us that scoffers are to arise, saying, "*Where is the promise of his coming?*" (2 Peter 3:4). And, truly, we have lived to see the day when men are saying, "*What has become of His promised Return,*" as Weymouth translates Peter's question.

Modernism, so blatant in its rejection of the revealed truth of the second coming, asserts that the apostles expected Christ in their day, but that they died disappointed. His coming must, therefore, be spiritualized. Christ comes in circumstances and death. Any providential happening is His advent. His personal return is despised, being spoken of as an "air-balloon theory." The ungodly may scoff at the truth, seeing that the coming of Christ will shorten their life of sin; although we have the conviction that there is no message that arouses the conscience of the lost like that of the return of the Savior in flaming fire to take vengeance on all those who reject the gospel. What one cannot understand is how professing Christians, with their Bible before them, can yet despise, discredit, and reject the advent testimony!

HASTEN HIS COMING

If the day of Christ's coming is fixed upon God's calendar, is it possible for Him to put it forward through any action of His own? Well, Peter tells us that we are not only to "look for," but "hasten the coming." (See 2 Peter 3:12, margin.) *"Expect and hasten the advent"* is Moffatt's translation. Weymouth, in expressing the same thought, refers us to John 8:56: *"Abraham your forefather exulted in the hope of seeing my day"*; literally "in order to see," as though the longing and the hope hastened the event.

We sometimes sing that stirring advent hymn:

Let all who look for, hasten
    That coming glorious day,
By earnest consecration.[21]

Yes, we can hasten Christ's coming by prevailing, unceasing intercession; unwavering faith in God's all-sufficiency; consecrated service for others; and sanctified living wherever our lot is cast.

ASHAMED AT HIS COMING

May God save each of us from this unworthy attitude: *"And now, little children, abide in him; that, when he shall appear, we may have confidence, and not be ashamed before him at his coming"* (1 John 2:28). Another rendering is: *"When he appears we may have confidence instead of shrinking from him in shame at his arrival"* (MOFFATT). Ashamed, we are told, means "to have the feeling which attends the performance of a dishonorable deed." Surely this solemn word ought to prepare us for the translation! May God save us from all dishonorable deeds, from all that is of the flesh and the world, from the least thing causing our faces to blush with shame as, for the first time, we gaze at our kind Lord. Let us so live as if ready to see Him at any moment! If we would be ashamed for Jesus to come and find us reading certain books, going to certain places, engaging in certain pleasures, then the sooner we quit these things the quicker shall we arrive at the correct advent attitude.

---

21. Daniel W. Whittle, "The Crowning Day," 1881.

5

THE SKY SYMBOL OF THE ADVENT

I am...the bright and morning star.
—Revelation 22:16

Christ presents Himself as *"Jesus...the bright and morning star"* (Revelation 22:16) or as it is also translated, *"The bright star of the morning"* (MOFFATT). In order to understand the full application of this glorious metaphor to Christ, we must give some consideration to the splendor of this sparkling planet in the dawning skies, ever proverbial for brightness and beauty.

By the bright and morning star we are to think of Venus, the brightest of the planets, and conspicuous for its wonderful brilliancy and beauty. The ancients knew this star under two aspects. First, as *Phosphorous*, or light-bearer, the morning star. Then as *Hesperus*, meaning evening, seeing that it is an evening star as well. Some connected it with the sun god, Apollo.

Under this striking figure Christ gives us a guarantee of the sovereignty of light over darkness when, with the children of the day, He will be manifested. Let us trace one or two characteristic features of this renowned star, which is a sun itself.

FORERUNNER OF THE DAY

As the Morning Star, Christ is the Harbinger, a prophecy, a Messenger of light and life, sustaining the same relation to His people as this star does to the world. It succeeds the darkness of night and ushers in another day, mingling its rays with the morning light. It heralds the approach of a new period of time and is therefore a fitting type of Him who is to lead us on to eternal day. Before long Christ is to chase away the dark night of sin and deliver His own from a world of gloom. The morning star is a harbinger to the greatest natural joy, namely, the rising of the sun, and Christ is the Harbinger of great joy to all nations. As His first coming heralded a new day, *"the dayspring [sun-rising] from on high hath visited us"* (Luke 1:78), so His second coming is to usher in the longed-for day. (See Romans 13:12; Isaiah 60:1–3.) And, as the morning star gives most light just before the break of day, we can apply the same thought to the bright witness of the church, which she ought to bear as she nears daybreak.

The morning star is likewise a terror to evil men and thieves, for when they see this sun of the morning rising they hasten to hide themselves lest the light of day overtake them and they are discovered. *"Men loved darkness rather than light, because their deeds were evil"* (John 3:19). It is thus that Christ is a terror to the wicked. Godless men would like to pluck this revealing star out of the divine firmament.

The morning star possesses an honorable name. It is called "Son of the Morning." Christ is the true Son of the Morning. Lucifer is a counterfeit. (See Isaiah 14:12.) Twilight may linger, but dayspring is at hand; as the Light of the World, the Son of God is coming to banish its darkness.

The morning star shines on, although it may be obscured by mists and fogs. Nothing can stay its circuit or shining. How suggestive all this is of Christ! Nothing demons or men can do will ever deter His progress. He will appear according to His promise.

GUIDE OF MARINERS

This star serves many great and beneficent purposes. It is a useful guide across the ocean. By its light, travelers are able to direct their course. And Christ is highly esteemed as a Guiding Star. Sailing homeward, we can steer a right course and avoid all the rocks and ultimately arrive in the heavenly port, when our eyes are on Jesus. What a blessed thing it is that light came into the world in the person of Him who is the bright and Morning Star! Shipwrecked souls, distressed and storm-tossed, can depend upon the Lord to guide them into a desired haven. Unless we are led by Him, we must perish in darkness.

MASTER OF PLANETS

The morning star is conspicuous for outstanding qualities:

1. *It is noted for its magnitude.* Astronomers account for this as the star of first magnitude. There is none like unto it. Thus is it with Christ. He exceeds angels and men. He surpasses all in His splendor. He is indeed supreme, incomparable, without an equal.

2. *It is noted for its rare beauty.* Some ancient writers have said that the morning star beautifies all the other planets. Christ's loveliness is extolled by Zechariah, "How great is His beauty…" (9:17).

3. *It is noted for its consideration.* Students of the heavenly bodies tell us that this star causes gentle storms in winter and moderate heat in summer. Well, Jesus is the Master of moderation! He knows how to temper the chastening we truly deserve. Knowing what we are able to bear, He adapts our necessary trials and testing accordingly.

4. *It is noted for its excellent properties.* We are also informed that this unique star sends forth beneficent influences toward the earth with its people and plants. Is not Christ the Source of all that is beneficial? All good and perfect gifts are from His bountiful hand. His goodness never fails!

5. It is noted for its double function. As an evening star as well as the morning star, Venus serves a double purpose. It is a guide by night and a herald of the coming day. Coming to Jesus, we discover Him to be our Alpha and Omega. He is the Author and Finisher of our faith. He is the First and the Last, and all in between. In the early morning of our life He is our Morning Star, waiting to guide us on our journey. When we reach the evening of life or as we encounter the night of trial, He is our *Hesperus* or evening star, also the One who is to banish all sorrow and gloom for His own.

THE MORNING STAR IS DISTINCT FROM THE SUN

The sun and the morning star are two distinct bodies, the latter being inferior to the former, yet dependent upon it. Christ, however, fulfills both types. He has a twofold relationship we must never lose sight of.

In His character as the Sun of Righteousness, He is connected with Israel whom He is to heal and bring into blessing. In His character as the Morning Star, He is associated with the church and His appearance for her before He rises as the Sun.

As the Sun of Righteousness, He is to arise with noonday glory and splendor for Israel's future bliss. As the Morning Star, He is to appear for His bride at least seven years before the millennium. The morning star appears just before the day and is seen only by watchers and early risers. If we would shine as a morning star here, we must bask in the light of Him who, as the Morning Star, will burst upon a dark world.

THE MORNING STAR GIVES ETERNAL LIGHT ONLY!

This glorious star can only reflect light to a visible world. What it constantly receives, it transmits. It has no light of its own. The little boy said that the stars were holes to let the glory through. But Christ imparts the eternal light, seeing He is the true light.

(See John 8:12.) And His glory radiates now, and will remain, even when the stars are no more.

THE MORNING STAR'S GLORY BECOMES DIM IN THE DAYTIME!

Venus is brightest at night. As day dawns, and the sun rises, this star loses its brilliance. Not so Christ! He is ever the same, day and night, summer and winter. Darkness and light are both alike to Him. (See Isaiah 60:20; John 1:5.)

THE MORNING STAR AWAITS DESTRUCTION

Peter tells us that the heavens, which include all the planets, are to be destroyed. God tells us that the heavens, in spite of their glory, are not clean in His sight. But Christ is absolutely pure, indestructible, and eternal, therefore let us hitch the wagon of our life to such a Star.

In conclusion, it must be observed that as the Morning Star, Christ is the pledge of the coming day, both for His own and for the ungodly, who love the darkness because of their evil deeds. He is the earnest of the sovereignty of light over darkness, when the children of the day are manifest, and shine as stars forever and ever.

6

RELATIONSHIPS IN THE LIGHT OF THE ADVENT

Unto the church...wait for his Son from heaven.
—1 Thessalonians 1:1, 10

The radical effect the truth of the second advent has upon our spiritual life is prominent in the Epistles. Repeatedly, we are reminded of the vital connection between the rapture and the quickening of the religious life of the church in general. If *conduct* is always affected by *conception*, what else can we expect if we scorn the great conception of the second advent with soiled garments and unlit lamp? If, as it has been said, "the power of any life lies in its expectancy," then those within the church, expecting their Lord's return, are those who live the most fruitful lives for Him.

THE THEME OF 1 THESSALONIANS

Thus, it is with such consideration in mind, that we now turn to the first epistle of Thessalonians, where the practical outworking of the advent is so clearly emphasized. It is affirmed by scholars that this epistle was the first New Testament book to be written, and is therefore the earliest piece of Christian writing in existence. As Paul's initial epistle, penned about AD 54, some twenty-one years after Calvary and sixteen years after the apostle's miraculous conversion on the Damascus road, it is indeed *The Epistle of Hope*. Circumstances regarding the foundation of this church at Thessalonica can be found in Acts 16 and 17. A revival broke out during one of Paul's evangelistic tours, and so great was the spiritual upheaval, that the world seemed to be *"turned…upside down"* (Acts 17:6).

Young though the church was, the main subject of Paul's preaching was the varied relationships of life in Christ in view of His return for His church. That the Thessalonians received the most accurate teaching concerning this truth is evident from what Paul states about no further need to dwell on such a revelation. (See 1 Thessalonians 5:1, 2.) He assumed that his converts had thoroughly apprehended and believed the doctrine taught them. *"If we believe…"* (1 Thessalonians 4:14).

We are reminded by one gifted expositor that the predominant theme of 1 Thessalonians is of a three-fold nature:

1. To strengthen the converts in the fundamental truths he has taught them during his month's ministry among them.

2. To encourage believers to seek after holiness of life, thus leading them from salvation to sanctification.

3. To comfort those who had lost loved ones, correcting an error regarding the happy dead.

Paul's epistles are saturated with the truth of the second coming of Christ. More than any other New Testament writer, he can be called the "apostle of the advent." Directly taught by the Holy Spirit, it is Paul who brings us a full revelation of the various aspects of our Lord's appearing. His two letters to the Thessalonians are particularly devoted to the church's rapture and earth's condition after the rapture. Taken together, these two remarkable epistles cover the two stages of Christ's return. The first epistle deals with and centers around our Lord's coming for His church. In the second epistle, we have characteristic features of the tribulation period.

Perhaps it has been noticed that at the end of each chapter in the first epistle to the Thessalonians, Paul concludes with some aspect of the second advent. He employs the blessed hope to give emphasis to *his* manifold exhortations, counsel, and warnings. Broadly, we can outline the five chapters thus:

Chapter 1 associates our salvation and patience with the return of Christ: *"For they themselves shew of us what manner of entering in we had unto you, and how ye turned to God from idols to serve the living and true God; and to wait for his Son from heaven, whom he raised from the dead, even Jesus, which delivered us from the wrath to come"* (vs. 9–10; see also Psalm 49:15).

Chapter 2 connects service and its reward with the coming of Jesus: *"For what is our hope, or joy, or crown of rejoicing? Are not even ye in the presence of our Lord Jesus Christ at his coming? For ye are our glory and joy"* (vs. 19–20).

Chapter 3 has conduct in view. Love, toward God and toward man, is prominent in this chapter: *"And the Lord make you to increase and abound in love one toward another, and toward all men, even as we do toward you: To the end he may stablish your hearts unblameable in holiness before God, even our Father, at the coming of our Lord Jesus Christ with all his saints"* (vs. 12–13).

Chapter 4 declares the second advent to be the spring of all our comfort: *"But I would not have you to be ignorant, brethren, concerning them which are asleep, that ye sorrow not, even as others which have no hope.... Wherefore comfort one another with these words"* (vs. 13, 18).

Chapter 5 outlines the character of the saint and reveals the sanctifying influence of the advent: *"And the very God of peace sanctify you wholly; and I pray God your whole spirit and soul and body be preserved blameless unto the coming of our Lord Jesus Christ"* (vs. 23).

Looking more closely at these five chapters we discover that Paul reminded the Thessalonians of a five-point relationship they had to preserve and practice in view of Christ's return.

1. AS A BELIEVER

For they themselves shew of us what manner of entering in we had unto you, and how ye turned to God from idols to serve the living and true God; and to wait for his Son from heaven, whom he raised from the dead, even Jesus, which delivered us from the wrath to come. (1 Thessalonians 1:9–10)

Here the believer is viewed as a *waiting one*, and *patience* appears to be the quality he must exhibit, seeing Christ is at hand. There are three words used by Paul to indicate a full-orbed life. They are *turn, serve*, and *wait*. Some turn but they do not serve. Others serve, but never learn to wait. Salvation, occupation, and expectation, however, go together. Going back to 1:3, we have an illuminating commentary on Paul's description of those Thessalonians that he was the means of winning to the Lord. He gives us a triad:

Their work of faith—turning to God from idols—past;
Their labor of love—serving the living and true God—present;
Their patience of hope—waiting for His Son from heaven—future.

Thus faith rests on the past; love works in the present; hope endures as seeing the future. The inclusion of "serving" proves that the advent does not cut the nerve of effort, but serves to strengthen one for all legitimate labor.

One reason why the church is flirting with the world is because she has put out of her mind (if ever she had it in there) the expectation of God's Son from heaven. She has activity in plenty, but the third part of her attitude is missing. It is said that Michelangelo, by his prolonged and unremitting toil upon frescoed domes, acquired such a habitual upturn of countenance that as he walked the streets, strangers, observing his bearing, set him down as somewhat visionary and eccentric. If, as professing Christians, our conversation is truly in heaven, our faces will be set toward heaven. Instead of having our eyes fastened on the ground, like the man with the muck rake Bunyan describes, we will walk the dusty paths of life with an upward look. Our eyes will be upon the coming dawn.

2. AS A WORKER

> *For what is our hope, or joy, or crown of rejoicing? Are not even ye in the presence of our Lord Jesus Christ at his coming? For ye are our glory and joy.* (1 Thessalonians 2:19–20)

Here the believer is presented as the *serving one*, and *joy* resulting from faithful ministry is prominent. One commentary has it, "It is the thought of presenting you to Him that thrills us with hope, joy, pride, the thought of wearing such a decoration before Him."[22] Paul is here declaring that at the judgment seat of Christ, he would be prouder of his converts than a king of his crown and a champion of his laurels. The apostle expresses a similar joy in 2 Corinthians 1:14 and Philemon 4:1.

There are crowns to earn, but this *"crown of rejoicing"* is the one acting as an incentive to service. What a thrill will be ours to realize that souls will be at the Bema because of our influence and testimony here below. Would it not make for a mighty revival if every believer truly lived and labored in the light of Christ's return? Are we as jealous as we should be over the winning of our own loved ones for the Lord? Mother, what about your daughter? Father, what about your boy? Christian worker, Sunday school teacher, what about those around you? Will others greet your Savior because of your faithful witness?

---

22. Charles John Ellicott, "Commentary on 1 Thessalonians 2:19–20," *Ellicott's Commentary for English Readers* (1905), BibleSupport.com, www.studylight.org/commentaries/ebc/1-thessalonians-2.html.

Possibly you have all the heart could wish for here on earth, for instance, a comfortable home, a well-appointed sphere, the absence of poverty or loneliness. But what of the future? Will you experience the joy and thrill of the apostle? Will there be any stars in your crown when at evening the sun goes down? Or will yours be a joyless meeting of the Savior; the reception of a starless crown; an entrance, empty-handed, into His presence? As we have not long to live, let us solemnly ask ourselves what joy and triumph will be ours when we see Jesus. God forbid that any of us should get just inside of glory, saved by faith, but nothing to our credit, no service to reward! May we hasten the crowning day by gathering the lost ones for whom the Savior died!

3. AS A BROTHER

And the Lord make you to increase and abound in love one toward another, and toward all men, even as we do toward you: To the end he may stablish your hearts unblameable in holiness before God, even our Father, at the coming of our Lord Jesus Christ with all his saints. (1 Thessalonians 3:12–13)

Here the believer is brought before us as a *loving one*, and *love*, toward God and man, is emphasized. "The Lord multiply you in love until you have enough and to spare of it."[23] Well, there is not too much to spare of love among Christians today! Paul's exhortation can be translated, "So that you may not only love one another abundantly, but all mankind."[24] Can we say that we are the true brother-kinsmen and friends of all Christ's little ones? What shame will be ours as we meet the gaze of Christ if we have not been kind to the household of faith! Paul points to his own example as he urges others to love. *"Night and day"* he thought of others (1 Thessalonians 3:10). *"Like a nursing mother cherishing her own*

---
23. Ellicott, "Commentary on 1 Thessalonians 3:12."
24. Ibid.

children" (1 Thessalonians 2:7 MOFFATT). And he here emphasizes brotherly love as the evidence of a life of holiness. A loveless heart can never succeed in the quest after holiness, for true love sanctifies the one who loves.

As the shadows gather, Paul would have us increase and abound in love or, as Dr. Weymouth puts it, have *"a growing and a glowing love."* Alas, the growth and glow of love is not being generally experienced by the Lord's people! Love's fruit is frosted. Paul prays that the Thessalonians might love one another in a superlative degree. He desired them to overflow in love. As we get nearer the return, it would seem as if the devil is active, drying up the spring of love, for never was there such an unloving attitude manifested among professing Christians. We sing about knowing each other better when the mists have rolled away, but why wait until the future for a full recognition? We must endeavor to know each other better here and now. In this epistle, Paul tells us that we must be at peace among ourselves. (See 5:13.) He urges the Thessalonians to greet one another with a holy kiss, which was a way of expressing love then. Now we feel more like kicking some Christians than kissing them! And yet a revival of love among God's people, in view of Christ's coming, would make for a mighty ingathering of lost souls. "*By this shall all men know that ye are my disciples, if ye have love one to another*" (John 13:35).

4. AS A SUFFERER

But I would not have you to be ignorant, brethren, concerning them which are asleep, that ye sorrow not, even as others which have no hope.... Wherefore comfort one another with these words. (1 Thessalonians 4:13, 18)

Here the believer is portrayed as the *weeping one,* and comfort, in view of the separations of life, is stressed by the writer. The Thessalonians were troubled over those who had died. Recently converted from their heathenism, they were still haunted by the pagan ideas of the future. A heathen inscription discovered in Thessalonica reads:

> After death no reviving,
> After the grave no meeting again.

And so Paul sends this letter assuring troubled hearts about the heavenly happiness and future resurrection of their holy dead. All who died in Christ are presently with Christ and will return with Him to assume glorified bodies. Thus all the sorrows, sufferings, and separations are lifted up and placed alongside of "the blessed hope," and thereby robbed of their sting. And because the unseen world is perpetually opening up to receive those we love, we continually need the comfort of Paul's advent truth. Amid the partings and farewells of life, so common in times of brutal war, we do not sorrow as others who have no hope. Weeping over those who have left us, we do not weep for them. A blissful reunion awaits the Lord's people.

> Some from earth, from glory some,
> Severed only 'til He come!"[25]

Alas, secular life today is almost as hopeless as the paganism Paul corrected. The multitudes have their attention fixed on the present world and studiously avoid all distraction of the future. Determined to have a good time now, they are willing to risk their chance in the world to come. The saints of God, however, sit loose to things of earth, seeing they may leave them at any moment to meet Jesus in the air. And as this old world ripens for judgment, let us comfort one another with the words of the coming shout and trump and voice.

---

25. Edward H. Bickersteth, "'Til He Come," 1861.

5. AS A SAINT

And the very God of peace sanctify you wholly; and I pray God your whole spirit and soul and body be preserved blameless unto the coming of our Lord Jesus Christ.

(1 Thessalonians 5:23)

Here the believer is brought before us as a holy one, and complete *sanctification* is the application Paul makes as he again stresses the coming arrival of Christ. And what a fitting climax this is for his advent epistle! Paul calls the saint to be saintly in life. He must be separated from sin, and dedicated to the service of the Lord. The question, then, of paramount importance is this: when Jesus comes, will He be pleased with the holiness of my life, the simplicity of my obedience, and the faithfulness of my service?

"*May the God of peace consecrate you through and through! Spirit, soul, and body, may you be kept without break or blame till the arrival of our Lord Jesus Christ!*" (MOFFATT). Without break! Without blame! Here are two suggestive thoughts based on the Scripture we have just quoted. "*Without break*" can indicate our relationship toward God. There must be no break, no rupture in our communion. We must strive after unbroken fellowship with the Lord. "*Without...blame*" can cover our relationships toward mankind. Fellowship, conduct, testimony must be in full harmony with our profession of holiness. We must be "consecrated through and through."

It will be noted that Paul thought of man as a three-part being, a trinity in unity. He is made up of spirit (life upward), soul (life inward), and body (life outward).

The body of the believer is the temple of the Holy Spirit and must therefore be free of all pampering and excess and neglect. Everything associated with such a temple should contribute to the glory of God. Holy lips should plead His cause, far and near. Holy hands should be continually active, doing good. Holy feet should move incessantly on errands of love and mercy.

The soul of the believer is the inner sanctuary where all the powers of thought and imagination should be as priests serving the Lord. All unholy, lawless, roving thoughts must be banished. Our conscience and self-life must be disciplined by God's Word and Spirit until they obey His dictates without a murmur.

The spirit of the believer must be guarded as the holy of holies. Pure worship and devotion and worthy thoughts of God must be cultivated. Worthy reverence and trust and conceptions of God must characterize the waiting, watching soul. If the saint is not to hang his head in shame and self-reproach as the Master asks questions of his secret soul, then every part of his complex nature must be sanctified as His coming draws near. With such a blessed hope in view he must be more holy. And what God commands, He graciously supplies. He calls us to be wholly sanctified, and *"Faithful is he that calleth you, who also will do it"* (1 Thessalonians 5:24). No wonder St. Augustine prayed, "Give what Thou commandest—then command what Thou wilt."

As mentioned previously, Massillon reminds us that "in the days of primitive Christianity it would have been deemed a kind of apostasy not to sigh for the return of the Lord." And Dr. Grattan Guinness says, "It cannot be denied that for three centuries the church held the doctrine of the Premillennial Coming of Christ. I think I have gone through all the writings of the Fathers for three centuries pretty carefully, and I do not know an exception unless it be (Origen) the only early writer who was often heterodox." If, then, the apostles and fathers used the coming of Christ as an incentive to holy living and diligent labor, is it not time for the church to return to the truth so prominent in their writings and witness? May grace be ours to hail the dawn as those who are fully right with God and with our fellow men!

7

GETTING READY FOR THE ADVENT

*Therefore be ye also ready:
for in such an hour as ye think not the Son of man cometh.*
—Matthew 24:44

As the sands of time are sinking and the dawn of heaven is about to break, it is incumbent upon us to give heed to Peter's injunction about the end of all things being at hand. By "the end" we can understand three consummations. First of all, there is the end of the church age at the return of the Lord in the air. And this sublime event, we feel, is not far distant. Then there is the end of the Gentile age, which will come when Christ appears on earth as King of Kings. Revealing Himself as the Prince of the kings of the earth, He will wind up the rule of all nations and introduce His own world-kingdom. The third "end" is the end of the world age which John describes in Revelation 20, when earth and heaven are to flee from the face of Him sitting on the throne. And by the phrase *"at hand"* in 1 Peter 4:7, we understand Peter to mean not the immediate cessation of any particular age, but that no known or predicted event intervenes.

But what does the apostle imply when he declares that the end of *"all things"* is at hand? What things are about to disappear? Well, all effective gospel ministry, soul-winning effort, personal testimony, and missionary activity are about to end! There is no immediate end to the sins and sorrows, griefs and groans of earth. Such an end is not yet! The end of our personal witness for Christ, however, is at hand, which means that we must redouble our energies, accelerate our speed, and pour our lives and substance into the service of winning the lost for the Savior before He returns for His own. And Peter leaves us in no doubt regarding the advent attitude. The narrative in 1 Peter 4 offers an illuminating commentary on how we should act in view of the end of this dispensation of the grace of God. We have, for example, the following eightfold glimpse of readiness:

1. SOBRIETY

But the end of all things is at hand: be ye therefore sober."
(1 Peter 4:7)

Here *"sober"* stands for self-control, discipline, and abstinence. As *"the end"* approaches, we must ask ourselves if there is anything we can do without. In evil days like our own, when lust is ministered to, and the majority are characterized by unbridled iniquity, the saint must not run to the same excess of riot. The rest of his time—and what time is left may be very short indeed—must not be lived in the flesh to the lusts of men, but to the will of God. Those around may think it strange if we turn from those sins that used to have a place in our life in time past. But now that separation is ours from the penalty and guilt of sin; by the grace of the Spirit the old fleshly habits are daily curbed and died to.

Are these critical days having a sobering influence on your life? Do you feel that a civilization so near the abyss demands that you live at your best? As society becomes more corrupt at the core, and old-time moral standards are set aside, are you becoming more puritan in life? The greatest rebuke to the sin of our age is holy living. Whatever the sin of Sardis was, it was made more conspicuous by the few within the city who had not defiled their garments.

(See Revelation 3:1–6.) Of course, Christian sobriety and godly self-control may call forth the hostility of carnal-minded people, but such is part of the price the child of God must pay for his allegiance to Him who remained God's untainted lily among surrounding thorns. Ours must be the determination to be different from others. By conduct and character, we must reveal to a sin-laden world that Christ is able to keep us in the world, and keep us from its evil.

2. PRAYERFULNESS

But the end of all things is at hand…watch unto prayer.

(1 Peter 4:7)

It is interesting to note that these words were written by the man who failed in the matter of prayer. Christ took Peter into Gethsemane with Him that he might have fellowship with his Master in prayer, but Peter slept when he should have travailed in prayer. And now Peter uses the very counsel of his Lord regarding watching unto prayer. Evidently he had profited by his failure. Watching here implies looking out for, or creating opportunities for, prayer. Taking advantage of, and ever preserving all set and accustomed times for prayer, we must endeavor to set aside more time for intercession. As the end approaches and the exigencies of war demand so much of one's time, we must guard the sweet hour of prayer. Satan is a past master at distraction and interruption when it comes to prayer. He realizes the power of persistent prayer.

Satan trembles when he sees,
The weakest saint upon his knees…[26]

And because, as the poet Alfred Tennyson said, "More things are wrought by prayer than this world dreams of," the

---
26. William Cowper, "What Various Hindrances We Meet," 1779.

chaotic condition of the world demands that the saints of God make a determined effort to focus earnest, believing intercession upon war-weary nations. The miracle of Dunkirk, when more than 300,000 Allied troops were evacuated from the beaches of Dunkirk, Belgium, where they were surrounded by German forces, proved what God is willing to do when a nation is driven to its knees. While we do not minimize the importance of all the Allied Nations produced in order to defeat the cruel forces of aggression, days of natural humiliation and prayer would take them farther along the road of victory. As of old, God waits to make bare His arm on our behalf—on the behalf of those people who are willing to depend upon Him.

3. FERVENT LOVE

But the end of all things is at hand.… Have fervent charity [love]. (1 Peter 4:7, 8)

Further back in 1 Peter 3:8, Peter exhorts us to exhibit love among ourselves as brethren. And here in the passage before us he reminds us that we must be *"keen to love one another"* (1 Peter 4:8 MOFFATT). It is somewhat profitable to trace the connection between the second advent and love. James tells us that because the Judge stands at the door, we are not to grudge or complain one against another. Alas, however, these last days are witnessing a lamentable absence of love and Christian kindness among ourselves as followers of Christ! The professed church is sadly divided. Bitter feuds, divisions, estrangements, and splits are all too evident. We may still sing, "We are not divided, all one body we," but this is only one lie we utter. Of course, mystically, the true church can never be torn asunder. All who are born again by the Spirit will ever remain one in Christ Jesus. In our attitude toward one another, and in our essential united witness, there can be, as unfortunately there is, a good deal of unhappy division.

A baptism of love, then, is one of the church's greatest needs in these days so heavy with opportunity. Well might we pray, "God, give us love!" Such a manifestation of love among us covers a multitude of sins, which means that if we truly love one another, as believers, we will not parade his or her faults but extol their virtues and maintain a discreet silence regarding their sins. This silence will not mean that we condone their failures. Loving those at fault, we will seek to help them in a personal way, pointing them to the only source of cleansing, namely, the blood of Christ. It is thus that our love will enable the one who has sinned to have his multitudinous sins effectively covered. Have you a somewhat hard, loveless attitude toward another Christian? Bow, and ask God for a loving, forgiving heart like His own!

4. UNGRUDGING HOSPITALITY

But the end of all things is at hand.... Use hospitality one to another without grudging. (1 Peter 4:7, 9)

Here is a good verse to use when anyone denying the second advent tells you that such a doctrine is not practical. Surely nothing could be more practical than that of showing hospitality one to another. And is there not a touch of irony in what Peter has to say about being hospitable *without a grudge?* We are not to be kind to others because we have to. Forced hospitality brings no satisfaction. If you see someone approaching your home and you say, "The last person I want to see just now," yet when the door opens you are all smiles and gushingly remark, "Well, Mrs. Smith, this is a pleasure! Come in; have a cup of tea" while inwardly you are boiling over with displeasure and everything you do to entertain your visitor is done with a grudge, then what a hypocrite you are!

Another writer tells us not to forget to entertain, especially strangers, seeing that they may be angels in disguise. (See Hebrews 13:2.)

One cannot resist giving Peter's practical exhortation a larger application. In this war-torn world, when multitudes are being driven from their homes and lands and face terrible starvation, America, the paradise of plenty, is proving herself to be a most hospitable nation. Refugees are coming here by the thousands, and the abundance of food friendly America possesses is being shared among those less privileged. And it is international hospitality without a grudge! When the end of this grim conflict is in sight, and the war resolves itself into a war of attrition, America will have a still greater part to play in the feeding and rehabilitation of the hungry and homeless throughout the world. And ungrudgingly her hospitality will be extended to the needy everywhere.[27]

5. FAITHFUL STEWARDSHIP

But the end of all things is at hand.... As every man hath received the gift, even so minister the same one to another.

(1 Peter 4:7, 10)

As the end of this age approaches, we are to use to the limit every God-given talent. Such, we take it, is the command of Peter. What we fail to realize is the fact that not only do we receive the Holy Spirit as a gift at regeneration, but from Him a distinct gift to be exercised in our service for the Lord. *"Every man hath received the gift.... Having then gifts differing"* (1 Peter 4:10; Romans 12:6). Have you discovered what your gift is, and are you using it to the limit? As a good steward, are you allowing the Spirit to possess fully His gift to you, and with it, to minister unto others? In the parable of the talents, the man with only one talent failed to multiply it. He hid it, we are told, in a napkin or handkerchief—the very

---

27. Editor's note: Herbert Lockyer wrote this circa 1945. Reference to the war and refugees reflect the crisis of World War II.

thing that should have been used to wipe the sweat from his brow as he worked with his talent for the good of others.

What a mighty force the church would become if only every believer could realize his or her gift and employ it with the ability God gives! Unused talents hinder the work of the Lord, aid the devil in his diabolical schemes, and help to keep multitudes of slaves in the prison house of sin. If you have been tempted to believe that you have no special gift to exercise in the Master's cause, get alone with Him today, and ask Him to show you what personal gift you received when He made you His child. And when you discover your talent, do not bury it. Put it to work. God has promised you the ability to use it wisely and well. In the little time left before Christ returns, the perilous condition of souls demands that any and all Spirit-given gifts must be liberated and made to contribute to the ultimate glory of God.

6. SUFFERING

But the end of all things is at hand.... Suffer as a Christian.
(1 Peter 4:7, 16)

Three times over in this chapter we have the word *"strange."* The world thinks it strange that we do not run after its pleasures. (See v. 4.) And the saints themselves are not to think it strange when the fiery trial is theirs. Suffering for Christ's sake must not be looked upon as some strange thing happening unto them. In these "suffering" verses, Peter reminds us that the Christian life is not a picnic but a battlefield. Living godly lives in Christ Jesus, we are bound to suffer in some way or another. And it would seem that as the nations hasten to their doom, hostility for the believer increases. Amid gathering gloom in the world, persecution has become the unwelcome lot of many saints, especially in those lands crushed underfoot by ruthless dictators.

Peter's homily on suffering has, as its key thought, the glory and privilege of bearing trial for Christ's sake. We are to rejoice when made a partaker of Christ's sufferings, and have happy hearts when reproached for His name. And when we suffer, it must be because we are Christians in life and work. Alas, we would never dream of suffering as murderers, thieves, evildoers, but we all come under the category of busybodies in other men's matters! Are you suffering as a Christian? If not, there is something wrong with your experience. You cannot live as unto the Lord without eliciting the reproach and ignominy of a Christ-hating world. As Christ's return draws near, faith is becoming a more precious possession to hold. Modernism and worldliness are foes of that which is positively Christian. On our part, however, there must be no compromise. No matter what it costs, we must be true to Christ's call and commission.

7. JUDGMENT OF THE CHURCH

But the end of all things is at hand.... Judgment must begin at the house of God. (1 Peter 4:7, 17)

Seeing that the church is a divinely created institution whose sacred task is fully and faithfully to represent God in a world of need, it is imperative for her to be adjusted to the mind of the Lord in order that His plans through the church might be realized. The primary mission of the church is that of evangelization. She was brought into being that she might continue the ministry of Christ, who came into the world to seek and to save the lost. Ceasing to evangelize, the church faces extinction. Any influence, therefore, responsible for the cessation of her passion to win the lost must be honestly dealt with. Church life and standards must be closely scrutinized and everything foreign to her walk and witness eliminated.

And the comparison Peter indicates between the judgment of the house of God, and the judgment of sinners, serves to emphasize the solemn necessity of the church's adherence to her divine pattern. *"If [judgment] first begin at us, what shall the end be of them that obey not the gospel of God?"* (1 Peter 4:17) And Peter's designation of the church is revealing. He calls her *"the house of God."* But how can God be present in any church where the virgin birth, deity, efficacious death, and physical resurrection of His Son are denied? Churches given over to modernism cease to function as churches after the New Testament order. And any so-called "house of God" where worldliness and social activities dominate the program is not a church, but simply a religious amusement and social center. In these last days, the church is confronted with the most glorious opportunity of her history. Before she can meet the challenge of the hour as terrible as any army with banners, she must repent and do her first works.

8. ENTIRE COMMITTAL

But the end of all things is at hand.... Commit the keeping of [your] souls to him. (1 Peter 4:7, 19)

Now that we have lived to see the day when every phase of life is undergoing a drastic change and disruption, separation, losses, and death have become common experiences, what is our source of consolation and guidance? "Change and decay in all around we see," but as children of God we have an *up-look* as well as an *outlook*. The outlook, as we write these lines, is indeed gloomy, and one would droop beneath the burden of things if it were not for the realization of God's omnipotence. These are certainly days when we must learn how to rest in the joy of what He is. Encouraging ourselves in God, we find our tasks somewhat lightened. As the faithful, unfailing Creator, God is well able to care for His own, and that in spite of all the necessities and complications a war-torn world produces. Ruling within the kingdom of men, He can care for His own and daily compass them about with songs of deliverance.

Some time ago the newspapers ran a story of a little London boy evacuated to Montreal, Canada. On his first night among strangers, when bedtime came round, he went to his knees to pray as he had been taught to do by Christian parents left behind in London. "Oh God," he prayed, "bless Mummy and Daddy and all my brothers and sisters. Keep them safe. And whatever you do, dear God, take care of Yourself, for if You are bombed, we're sunk." Well, is it not blessed to know that we trust One who cannot be reached or influenced by the tides of war? The Lord God Omnipotent reigns; therefore, let us commit the cares, trials, and needs of our entire life into the hands of One who can cause all things to work together for our good.

8

THE ANTEDILUVIANS AND THE ADVENT

But as the days of Noah were,
so shall also the coming of the Son of man be.
—Matthew 24:37

The solemn declaration of Christ that the days of Noah are to be reproduced as the time of His advent to the earth draws near, bids us return to a consideration of those influences leading up to and responsible for the flood, in which *"all in whose nostrils was the breath of life, of all that was in the dry land, died"* (Genesis 7:22). Corruption and violence exhausted the forbearance of God toward earth-dwellers, and caused Him to send His righteous judgment upon the godless of Noah's age. Patiently God bore with the wickedness of that time, but ultimately, His gleaning sickle removed the generations which were so destitute of any redeeming grace.

It is this story of terrible doom which our Lord links to an urgent warning for those who will witness the closing scenes of this Gentile age, when a reproduction of Noah's days is to be experienced.

> *But as the days of Noah were, so shall also the coming of the Son of man be. For as in the days that were before the flood they were eating and drinking, marrying and giving in marriage, until the day that Noe entered into the ark, and knew*

not until the flood came, and took them all away; so shall also the coming of the Son of man be. (Matthew 24:37–39)

Here our Lord is making it clear that the same intense worldliness, the same inability to care for the things of God, the same ignorance regarding impending judgment characterizing the antediluvians, these will likewise describe the world as Christ begins those judgments ending in the glory of His appearing.

The question before us in this chapter is whether the same fatal influences Noah encountered are presently affecting the world's masses. If the conditions prevalent in Noah's day are universally characteristic of our time, as we are rapidly drifting to a catastrophe as terrible as the flood, then it is imperative to cry aloud and warn both saint and sinner of impending doom.

In his masterly work on *Earth's Earliest Ages*, George Pember indicates several causes necessitating the flood, and we purpose adopting and adapting some of Pember's points as we endeavor to understand the signs of the times indicating the hurried approach of the great and stupendous climax of Christ's return.[28]

A PARTIAL VIEW OF GOD

One cannot study Genesis 5 and 6 without realizing that the God of Enoch and of Noah was not the God of the masses. There was a growing tendency to worship God as Elohim, that is, as a Creator so beneficent in His provision. Somehow He was not adored as Jehovah, the covenant God of mercy, dealing with sinners appointed to destruction and providing a ransom for them. Then the multitudes went the way of Cain. Their faith was in a God lenient with sin—in a God satisfied with human merit. Cain represents the natural man who believes in religion without sacrifice. Abel, of course, was a man of the altar.

---

28. See George Pember, *Earth's Earliest Ages* (London: Hodder and Stoughton, 1889).

What is the modern view of God and of His beloved Son? Has not modernism taught us to look upon God as one so supreme, kind, and benevolent? His love is emphasized at the expense of His justice. He is not presented as majestic in holiness, hating sin, and pronouncing a total depravity requiring the shedding of blood so that sinners can be reconciled to Him. As for Christ, He is presented as a wonderful man, whose wise philosophies and exemplary life should be followed. His deity and authority are taken from Him. Christ is humanized and man is deified. The Son of God is made less than He is, and man is made more than he is, and such reversals have nullified the sacrifice on the cross on behalf of sinners.

With the advance of civilization, intellectual pride and self-satisfied attainment have taken the place of Christ. Man is his own god. But amid a departure from the true revelation of God just as great as that of Noah's day, we must vindicate His claims as Redeemer, Lord, and Judge.

LAXITY OF THE MARRIAGE LAW

There are those scholars who affirm that it was a free, illicit love that helped to fill the earth with corruption in the days of Noah. The daughters of men cohabited with the sons of God, or angels of God, as it can be interpreted. Pember and others insist that Genesis 6:1–2 proves that women broke and disregarded the sacred bond of marriage. Association with fallen spirits made possible the giants whose strength was used against God. The mighty men of renown with their remarkable muscular power helped to fill the earth with violence.

Coming to our Lord's description of Noah's day, He speaks of the people marrying and giving in marriage. One writer suggests that the latter phrase, *"giving in marriage"* (Matthew 24:39) can be made to mean "exchanging in marriage"—the swap of husbands and wives for which Hollywood is conspicuous. And this growing looseness of the marriage tie is a matter of serious concern. There are those, like Bertrand Russell, who openly affirm that wedlock need not be for life but only for as long as agreeable to the contracting parties. Thus companionate marriages are advocated, with their convenient and legalized state of adultery. Birth control, with its often inhuman contraceptive methods, is causing the foul breath of pollution to cover the land. The same can be said for the murderous practice of abortion.

In the days of Noah, God was obliged to sweep all off of the face of the earth because of the unnatural union between fallen angels and women. In these days this very feature is again prominent, for in Spiritism, mediums enter into spiritual marriages. Spirits make love to these women and they enter into a contract whereby they call themselves the brides or spiritual wives of angelic beings. Sydney Watson, in his book, *Mark of the Beast*, hints that possibly the superman, the terrible man of sin, will come out of one of these spiritualistic alliances, and that he will be another being similar to the mighty men of renown who perished in the flood.

PROGRESS OF CIVILIZATION

Genesis 4 records a vast and rapid development of arts and knowledge. As civilization expanded, men became more cultured and clever. Communities and cities sprang into being, and the invention of mechanical appliances, along with the introduction of sciences and music, kept pace with a growing race. The construction of the ark reveals that man knew all the essential features of building in Noah's day. Archeological discoveries prove that at about this Noahic period, man had attained a high degree of civilization which has hardly been superseded.

Coming to our time, we know that the last generation has witnessed a colossal expansion of arts and sciences, as well as the production of inventions greatly benefiting civilization. Man has been able to unravel the secrets of nature as never before. We stand aghast at his uncanny discoveries. Electricity, radio, television, telephotography, automobiles, airplanes, and a hundred other wonderful benefits to which we have become accustomed, are evidences of marvelous progress in many realms. What a tragedy it is that almost all the advantages of science are being harnessed to the chariot of war!

But as in the days of Noah, when men began to depend upon their own resources and to be carried away in arrogance over their own achievements, so now the multitudes carelessly settle down to the comforts, conveniences, and indulgences of this luxurious age. As the people destroyed by the flood were self-contained and occupied with their own intellectual pursuits, ignoring the claims of the God they lived and died without, so men today are animated by the same spirit. Having gained back part of his supremacy over nature which he lost by the fall, man is content with the benefit of these secrets he has wrested from the bosom of the unknown. His discoveries are making him independent of God. And his very culture, upon which he prides himself, is not only unchristian in certain directions but positively anti-Christian. Man is out to build his Tower of Babel over again. With his self-deification, man is endeavoring to sit in the place of God. The Bible warns us, however, that amid all the discoveries of our age, amazing though they be, the tempest of God's fury is to break, causing the loftiness of man to be brought to nothing.

> *For the day of the* Lord *of hosts shall be upon every one that is proud and lofty, and upon every one that is lifted up; and he shall be brought low: and upon all the cedars of Lebanon, that are high and lifted up, and upon all the oaks of Bashan, and upon all the high mountains, and upon all the hills that are lifted up, and upon every high tower, and upon every fenced wall, and upon all the ships of Tarshish, and upon all pleasant*

> *pictures. And the loftiness of man shall be bowed down, and the haughtiness of men shall be made low: and the* LORD *alone shall be exalted in that day.* (Isaiah 2:12–17)

There was no church in Noah's time, in the accepted sense of the term, yet people had a semblance of religion. They called upon, or called themselves by, the name of the Lord. (See Genesis 4:26.) There was a nominal worship of God, but the religion of that age was without blood and power. Both Enoch and Noah walked with God. They were saints. And being men of the altar, their lives were distinct. Being perfect in their generation means that they were not allied with, and consequently not contaminated by, their surroundings. But the antediluvians were good mixers. They tried to combine God and mammon, and, as a result, perished in the flood.

Is there not another parallel here? Have we not lived to see the day when man is content to clothe himself with the garment of religious devotion and at the same time plunge into all the fun and frivolities of the world? All this talk about a fallen humanity and man being corrupt enough to require a Savior is relegated to the antiquated theology of the dim ages of the past. The practical teaching of many religious leaders is that God is fairly well satisfied with man and troubles little about his sin. God is surely highly appreciative of man's works, virtues, bold deeds, and intellectualism. Those who argue thus are assured that they will never hear the dread sentence, *"Thou fool, this night thy soul shall be required of thee"* (Luke 12:20). Would that we could get the multitudes to realize the terrible reality of judgment ahead for them unless they truly repent!

There is, of course, the broader alliance of the church with the world and its ways. The miracle of Pentecost was the placing of the church in the world as a witness. Satan's masterpiece is the reversal of the divine order, for he has succeeded in placing the world in the church. And it is this worldly compromise that has robbed the church of her influence over the world. All novelties have been tried by the church to attract and hold people. It might be a novelty to try the gospel and see how it works.

INCREASE OF POPULATION

A rapid increase of population is expressly taught in the words, *"when men began to multiply"* (Genesis 6:1). Doubtless it was this fact that accentuated the wickedness and peril of those apostate days. Growth of population ever tends to intensify sin. There are certain vices peculiar to crowded districts and countries. Where men and women are numerous, they can support each other in rebellion and godlessness and are prone to become more daring and more defiant.

The world has never witnessed such a vast assembly of human life as it now holds. And with this rapid increase, men have learned how to act together. Vast organizations have sprung into existence. Densely-thronged communities have become strongholds of rationalism, communism, and paganism. Humanity is fast reaching a second Babel and the Lord will shortly descend to confound and destroy the godless hordes of earth. Would that the millions of earth, as sheep without a shepherd, turn to the Savior! God grant us compassionate hearts as we look out upon earth's uncounted multitudes.

REJECTION OF A GOD-INSPIRED WITNESS

Another characteristic feature of Noah's day was the persistent rejection of this preacher's message. First of all, there was the powerful appeal of Enoch as he called a declining age to repentance. His threatenings of judgment were spurned. As day followed day and no sign of predicted doom appeared, men lost all fear and became incapable of response to the Lord's appeal through Enoch.

God in His goodness, however, sent another witness. Noah succeeded Enoch and for one hundred and twenty years preached divine righteousness. But his testimony and holy living, like that of his predecessor, were rejected. The far-off terrible flood was real to Noah—more real than the life around him. We can imagine him being scoffed at, but Noah was indifferent to all the gibes, seeing he believed God's wrath would be manifested against his corrupt age.

Today there are those who whitewash this wonderful age. Attention is drawn to the unique advances in the realm of art, commerce, and education. Alas, however, our much-vaunted civilization is committing suicide! And when we speak of universal judgment, cultured—but Christless—people who argue against the miraculous, declare that a flood such as Noah experienced is contrary to all the known laws of nature. It is more than likely, as Noah kept on predicting the flood and building his ark in the face of arrogant contempt, that the people came to look upon him as a weak-minded fanatic, a preacher void of intellect and therefore unworthy of notice. But Noah went on with his preaching and building.

And what is the true condition of things today? Sinners are gospel-hardened and religious sinners are truth-hardened. In spite of earnest preaching and multiplicity of urgent appeals, and organizations touching every section of society with Bibles, tracts, and booklets, the multitudes appear to be more indifferent than ever. Sinners are harder to reach and win. And now, with the preoccupation of prosperity, Christian work has become very difficult. But increasing indifference on the part of the masses to the gospel must not deter us. Noah went on building his ark, even though none apart from his own immediate circle heeded his warnings. Once the door of that ark was shut, and the floods began to rise, frightened crowds fought for admission, but the separation had been made and the day of vengeance had commenced.

And our Lord in His comparison shows that the world will continue unconscious of its doom down to the very last. Light continues to shine, but the darkness comprehends it not. As the antediluvians pursued their revelry and merriment unconscious of their terrible end, so Christ declares that His coming in judgment will overtake the godless with the same suddenness. And as we realize that the end of this day of grace is near, we must labor on, never ceasing to warn the multitudes around who are absorbed in their worldliness. They may count our witness old-fashioned and out of touch with the modern world, but knowing that the oft-rejected Savior will soon mow down the rebellious with His scythe of judgment, we must urge the souls around to repent and believe.

In his unique *Expositions*, Dr. Alexander MacLaren has a chapter on Noah as "A Saint Among Sinners," in which he gives emphasis to the following appeal:

> The far-off flood was more real to [Noah] than the shows of life around him. Therefore he could stand all the gibes, and gave himself to a course of life which was sheer folly unless that future was real.... For a hundred and twenty years the wits laughed and the "common sense" people wondered, and the patient saint went on hammering and pitching at his ark. But one morning it began to rain; and by degrees, somehow, Noah did not seem quite such a fool. The jests would look rather different when the water was up to the knees of the jesters; and their sarcasms would stick in their throats as they drowned. So it is always. So it will be at the last great day. The men who lived for the future, by faith in Christ, will be found out to have been the wise men when the future has become the present, and the present has become the past, and is gone forever, while they who also had no aims beyond the things of time, which are now sunk beneath the dreary horizon, will

awake too late to the conviction that they are outside the ark of safety, and that their truest epitaph is "Thou fool!"[29]

SATANIC ACTIVITY

It would seem as if the most terrible and fearful characteristic feature of Noah's time was the unlawful appearance among men of beings from another sphere, and the unlawful intercourse of these citizens of the air with the women of the earth. The general interpretation of Genesis 6:2 is that *"the sons of God"* were the pious descendants of Seth and *"the daughters of men"* the offspring of Cain. However, there is no proof that this is so, seeing no special class is mentioned.

"The sons of God," we take it, is a phrase describing the angels that kept not their first estate. Peter connects the angels that sinned with Noah and the flood. (See 2 Peter 2:4–5.) And going after *"strange flesh"* (see Jude 6–7) can indicate the desire of the fallen angels for the daughters of men. What a fatal league!

Thus the days of Noah were marked by remarkable activity of lost spirits, all of whom were inspired and energized by the archenemy of God and man. And for such an unholy affiliation and corrupted atmosphere, God had to come down and cleanse the earth with a deluge. What of the last days of this gospel era? Are we not witnessing the revival of satanic activity in all shapes and forms? Hell is closing in on earth, and earth is again ripening for judgment. These are days of intense conflict. The struggle, whether individually or internationally, is not against flesh and blood, but against principalities, powers, rulers of the darkness of this world, and spiritual wickedness in high places. (See Ephesians 6:12.) The days of terror are fast coming when Satan and his evil host are to

---

29. Alexander Maclaren, "The Saint Among Sinners," *Expositions of Holy Scripture*, Biblesupport.com, www.studylight.org/commentaries/mac/genesis-6.html.

be swept from their aerial abode, and woe to the inhabitants of the earth when the devil is among them.

Already we live in a devilized world. Knowing that his time is short, Satan is increasing his pressure. Spiritism, for example, which in some cases adherents subscribe to the belief they can communicate with the dead, is spreading with remarkable rapidity and because of the widespread influence of this false cult, the world is full of evil spirits who impersonate the dead. The apostate religion of Spiritualism holds its devotees solely by the exhibition of the miraculous. In Revelation 12, we have the open interference of evil spirits with our present world. When Satan is confined to the narrow bounds of earth, there will be witnessed lying wonders, and with such the preparation for unparalleled woe and tribulation. Doomed since his deposition, the devil is to break every restraint and recklessly gratify every evil desire, and once more cover the earth with corruption and violence. And that Satan is unusually active is evidenced by the fact that he has loosed multitudes of demons to bring about universal apostasy and the establishment of a general communication between the powers of darkness and the children of disobedience.

Beloved, the armies of hell are on the march. Corruption, violence, vandalism, robbery, hijacking, kidnapping, tragic sectarian conflict, and the shadow of strife between blacks and whites, are all alike inspired of Satan, the archenemy of God and of mankind. Sinister forces are rampant. Earth is being prepared for tangible forms from the unseen world. And amid gathering darkness, our solemn task is to go on with the ark building. We must preach the truth, walk with God, live for eternity. When the floods of judgment again fall upon a guilty earth, we shall be safe in the divine ark, away from the fearful carnage a devil-driven world deserves. As the Lord tarries, may our voices vibrate with the passion of Calvary, as we assiduously warn sinners to flee the coming wrath and judgment.

9

PORTENTS OF THE GREAT TRIBULATION

For then shall be great tribulation, such as was not since the beginning of the world to this time, no, nor ever shall be.
—Matthew 24:21

In all our study of prophecy we must not forget that Christ may be here at any moment. It is within the range of possibility that the saints may be called away before another sunrise. The troubled condition of the world indicates that the Lord is at hand. We are living in the closing period of the wonderful church age and signs abound that her translation is near. While no man has any knowledge of the exact day of Christ's return, all the saints believing such an evident New Testament truth realize that the blissful event cannot be far away.

While we do not believe that the church is to pass through the great tribulation, we do affirm that coming events have the power to cast their shadows beforehand. And, if we have any discernment of the signs of the times, we must see in them a preview of the terrible drama about to be unfolded.

One marked feature of the tribulation era will be a remarkable unanimity among the forces. Federation, combination, and unity are to characterize all phases of life. "*These have one mind, and shall give their power and strength unto the beast*" (Revelation 17:13). A similar state, in which there is no division, but perfect amalgamation, is emphasized in the further words, *"For God hath put in their hearts to fulfil his will* [the will of the beast], *and to agree, and give their kingdom unto the beast"* (Revelation 17:17). And, as our day is one of unions, alliances, federations, and combines, it is not hard to detect the prophetic trend of world affairs.

The grim shadow of the tribulation period can be traced in three directions. First of all, in the *commercial world* there has been a rapid development of combines and trusts among capital and labor. The last fifty years have developed the genius of getting together. *"Gather ye together first the tares"* (Matthew 13:30). Thus, in labor, we have the grouping of millions into organizations created to preserve their interests. Then we have the centralization of industries enriching to a few, impoverishing to many. And so individual interest is being eliminated. This industrial federation is to develop with the advent of the Antichrist, when all private concerns will cease and everything will be unified under his controlling hand. *"And that no man might buy or sell, save he that had the mark, or the name of the beast, or the number of his name"* (Revelation 13:17). Then, those failing to acknowledge the symbol of autocratic control must perish from starvation. And, if present-day dictators have their way, this state of things is to be instituted.

The *political world* is also dominated by the desire for alliances. Thus we read of annexes, incorporation, and submergence of small nations by larger, more masterful nations. Generally speaking, all the nations are now in two groups, namely, the Allied Nations and the Axis Powers. Constantly the map is being reshuffled, preparing the way, we believe, for the formation of the Northern Confederacy on the one hand, and the revived Roman Empire on the other.[30] The perfect federation of all nations will not be experienced until Christ returns to

---

30. Editor's note: Herbert Lockyer wrote this circa 1945. Reference to the Allied Nations and Axis Powers reflect struggle for dominance near the end of World War II.

fashion the kingdom of this world into His own world-empire. (See Revelation 11:15.)

The *religious world* has also caught the world's fever for combination and union, affording another shadow of the tribulation days, when one universal church, apostate in character, will control all things religious. And movements toward union command the time and energies of the majority of church leaders. The time has come, they say, to banish all our differences and present one common front. Too long have theological barriers divided us. Let us get together and have one great religious fraternity. And it is in this spirit of goodwill that Jews, Catholics, and Protestants are fraternizing. But one is suspicious of such combination, remembering the story of the wolf in Little Red Riding Hood, who ultimately devoured everything coming in his way.

Paul, however, declares that Christ alone is able to unify all things in Himself. (See Ephesians 1:10, 19.) We can only be one in Christ Jesus. Therefore accepting, as we must, the unity of believers, we totally reject the union of denominations and opposing religious forces, which union is out to produce strange bedfellows. But let us not be blind to the fact that the one, united church is coming. When the true church has left the world, the Antichrist, along with the False Prophet, will be responsible for the apostate church, already named for us as *"the great whore.... THE MOTHER OF HARLOTS"* (Revelation 17:1, 5).

Our Lord upbraided the Pharisees for being able to judge what kind of weather they were to have but being altogether lacking in spiritual perception to discern the signs of the times. (See Matthew 16:3.) Signs, we take it, are related to what will happen after the church has gone. The church herself is signless and timeless. She is not looking around for signs, but listening for the sound of the descending Lord. The shadow of these signs, however, is falling across the earth, and it is our responsibility to detect and interpret the shadows.

WORLD SIGNS

Taking the Bible as our infallible guide and comparing it with the happenings of our time, we instinctively feel that some kind of a climax is at hand. Even men who are worldly in outlook tell us that international events are heavy with significance. Well, let us enumerate a few biblical descriptions of this end-time period and see if we can trace any comparison in our fast-moving age!

1. NATIONAL CATASTROPHES

Our Lord's Olivet discourse in Matthew 24 has been interpreted in various and conflicting ways. One understanding of the chapter, spoken from the Mount of Olives, is that it describes the condition of things on the earth as the time draws near for the Lord to return to the Mount of Olives as predicted in Zechariah 14:4, *"His feet shall stand in that day upon the mount of Olives."* It would seem as if verses 4–14 take us up to the end of the first half of the tribulation. While, of course, it is perfectly legitimate to make any application of the portion we like, we must always be careful to place its direct interpretation first. If, then, we are here given a panorama of events that will characterize the earth after the removal of the church, surely it is evident that the shadow of these terrible events is already darkening the world.

War: *"And ye shall hear of wars and rumours of wars…"* (Matthew 24:6).

More than two thousand years ago the Prince of Peace was crucified, and the earth has been red with human blood ever since. What wars have come and gone, transforming the world into a vale of tears! But we have been permitted to witness the bloodiest war in history, namely, World War II. Never has there been such desolation, destruction, and death. Civilization is committing suicide. And yet, in spite of what rulers planned in the direction of a post-war peace, we know that bloodier conflicts are to come. The battle of Armageddon, the most dreadful the world will ever know, is yet ahead. Presently, there is distress among the nations, with perplexity, but what will the earth be like when our Lord begins to overturn, according to His long-predicted Word?

The threat of global war in our time is indeed fearful, disrupting life for men and women everywhere, but the end is not yet. Perhaps we are at the beginning of sorrows. Well, if earth's present fiery baptism is the beginning, what will the development and end be like? How grateful we ought to be that, as the saved of the Lord, we will not experience the horror of the tribulation!

Famine: *"...there shall be famines..."* (v. 7).

From early Bible days, famine has stricken peoples in different parts of the world. Today, as never before, millions are starving, so much so that dogs, cats, and even rats are being eaten. The terrible experiences of countless numbers in different parts of the world are beyond our imagination to conceive. The rulers of the United Nations are already haunted by the picture of the conditions that will prevail if famine spreads. Small nations, conquered by heartless dictators, have been bled white. Already destitute, these beggared peoples face almost total extermination unless relief reaches them.

Pestilences: *"there shall be...pestilences"* (v. 7).

Pestilences are ever the scavengers of famine. They are never far away when destitution is abroad. With the lack of nutritious food, physical resistance to germs and microbes is weakened, and then it is that grievous pestilences come in for the kill. Are not our hearts saddened by the dread diseases and fevers that have overtaken so many in blood-soaked countries! A grim shadow, surely, of what God will permit the earth to endure when His judgments are abroad, and so much of its surface is to be scorched by fire.

Earthquakes: *"there shall be...earthquakes, in divers places"* (v. 7).

We take it that these particular earthquakes will come in unaccustomed places, as well as in countries in which they usually happen. A somewhat recent survey of the phenomenon of earthquakes has revealed that the earth has suffered more quakes during the last fifteen years than in all the rest of its existence. But disastrous as earthquakes have been within the last year or two, they will be mere tremors in comparison with the *"great earthquake, such as was not since men were upon the earth, so mighty an earthquake, and so great"* (Revelation 16:18).

Thus, the rumblings in nature and physical disturbances, experienced from time to time, indicate that even creation herself is getting ready for the coming of the Creator. And once He liberates the imprisoned forces of nature, woe to the inhabitants of the earth.

2. INCREASING WORLDLINESS

In the prophet Isaiah's judgment upon Babylon, he speaks of her as given to pleasures and dwelling carelessly. (See Isaiah 47:8.) Is such a description not characteristic of our day and generation? Was there ever a time when people were so pleasure-loving and utterly careless regarding the spiritual and eternal welfare of their souls? Paul reminds us that in the last days men are to be lovers of pleasure more than lovers of God. (See 2 Timothy 3:2, 4.) And what colossal sums are being spent, even in these days of misery in other parts of the world, on pleasures of all kinds! The tragedy is that Sunday, our Lord's Day, has become conspicuous as a day for sport and amusement. Whatever we must sacrifice, let it not be our pleasure. In spite of desolation all around, the show must go on. Is it any wonder that anguish overtakes any nation wasting its substance in riotous living? Think of the billions that people spend on the movies, baseball games, worldly entertainments, and the mere pittance they give, in comparison, for their spiritual and cultural interests!

3. ABOUNDING INIQUITY

We live in an age of suggestiveness. Widespread wars tend to let down the bars of moral standards. The impact of immorality is felt on every hand. Our Lord declared that iniquity is to flourish when all spiritual restraints have been removed. Evil men and seducers are to grow worse and worse. (See Matthew 24:12; 2 Timothy 3:13.) And the lamentable increase of suicides, mental health issues, divorces, crime, murder, and other hideous scenes reveals that society is becoming more corrupt and that lust is being ministered to in many ways. Birth control, the undress of our times, and other creations of hell, are helping to drive the country off the purity standard. The diabolical schemes some men devise are enough to make angels blush. But what will it be like when the church, the salt arresting so much of the world's corruption, is removed and the Man of Sin brings to a climax the sin of man?

4. RESTRAINED LAWLESSNESS

It is evident to the most casual observer that a hidden hand is paralyzing the life and peace of nations and men. *"The mystery of iniquity doth already work"* (2 Thessalonians 2:7). And present-day international unrest and disorder constitute another shadow of the terrible era when seething, unrestrained forces will make for the overthrow of all order and authority. While, of course, it may be deemed unpatriotic to say anything about Russia, one wonders if, when she becomes a world power, she will not become a world menace. If her communistic ideology remains unchanged, then sorrows will be multiplied, even for the nations presently allied with Russia, whose atheistic doctrines have never been abandoned.[31]

---

31. Editor's note: This was written circa 1945. It is noteworthy that, indeed, Lockyer's concerns were realized in the middle to latter half of the twentieth century when Russia's communistic ideology wrecked the lives of many of its citizens, including its Christians.

5. JEWISH ACTIVITIES

The Jews are God's index finger when it comes to prophecy. When, as the fig tree, Israel blossoms, then we know that Christ's coming is near, even at the doors. (See Matthew 24:32–33.) Nationally, intellectually and socially the Jews have awakened. Some of the most outstanding figures in art, literature, music and science, as well as commerce, are Jews. Key positions are held by many of the sons of Jacob.

Having been harassed and persecuted by Hitler, the modern pharaoh, the Jews have stood at his grave, even as they have stood at the tomb of all previous persecutors of their race. The Jews are indestructible. All the predictions of their glorious future heritage will be fully realized. Soon the times of the Gentiles will cease, and Israel will occupy in its entirety the land which is hers by divine right and gift.

CHURCH SIGNS

When we speak of the church, we refer to it in the general sense, meaning the visible, organized church. We preserve the distinction between the *organism* and the *organization*. A person can be in one and not in the other. With enthusiasm people can work *for* the faith without being *in* the faith. *"Examine yourselves, whether ye be in the faith"* (2 Corinthians 13:5). The church as a living organism will be caught up to meet the Lord in the air, but the church as an organization will remain on the earth and quickly become the apostate church already described. Let us now endeavor to trace the shadow of this coming apostate condition.

1. SPIRITUAL DECLINE

Without doubt, the church has left her first love. Leaves of profession are in abundance, but fruit, satisfying to the Master, is lacking. The love of many within her borders has waxed cold.

Almost all the Protestant denominations report lamentable decreases in church membership and Sunday school attendance. At the British Methodist Congress held as far back as July 1938, the president, deploring the lapse of people from public worship, remarked that the great Methodist Church had 320,000 less Sunday school attendants than six years previous when the union of various branches of Methodism took place.

Well, what else can we expect but spiritual decline when modernistic teaching, a worldly atmosphere, unspiritual ministry, and an unregenerated membership have been tolerated?

2. POWERLESS RELIGION

In describing the church in the last days, Paul declared that she would have a form of godliness, but be destitute of power. (See 2 Timothy 3:5.) And what impotence is hers! Sound, it may be, in respect to theology. *But sound asleep!* She has a name that lives, but she is dead. The church faces the unhappy plight of the world, utterly unable to stem the rising tide of paganism. Churches appear emptier than they were. Split by division, cursed with a dead orthodoxy, and saturated with worldly methods of interest and support, the church is a shadow of her former self. The great godless world passes by her doors untouched, unreached by her religious activities. Would that she would rouse herself and become as terrible as an army with banners!

3. APOSTATE TEACHING

It is clear from various Scriptures that the end of the church age is to be characterized by a falling-away of a pronounced character. Leaders and teachers are to abandon a position once held. In the latter times, some are to depart from the faith. (See 1 Timothy 4:1.) Men are to turn from the truth to (and seek to turn the truth into) fables. (See 2 Timothy 4:3–4.) The day has arrived when men are not valiant for the truth upon the earth. (See Jeremiah 9:3.) If one clings to foundational truths, he is scorned as being old-fashioned, antiquated, behind the times, ignorant, or unenlightened. Jesus asked the question, *"when the Son of man cometh, shall he find [the] faith on the earth?"* (Luke 18:8). Faith, He will find! Plenty of it—in this cult and the other. But *the* faith will be a precious commodity.

Is it not tragic that so many young people go to our colleges and seminaries and earn degrees and lose their convictions? What else can we expect but an impoverished church, when so many whose sacred task it is to train her ministers are so modernistic in their theology! We have no right to give a cent of our money for the support of any institution, church, or minister who denies the faith once delivered unto the saints!

4. SEDUCTIVE DOCTRINES

The last fifty years have witnessed an alarming increase of non-Christian religions. So-called Christian churches may be on the decline, but false cults, some of them "Christian" in name, are thriving. And the sad feature is that these cults thrive on those in Protestant churches who lack a spiritual experience and spiritual perception. *"Now the Spirit speaketh expressly, that in the latter times some shall depart from the faith, giving heed to seducing spirits, and doctrines of devils"* (1 Timothy 4:1–2). Spiritualism, or Spiritism, astrology, and forms of mysticism are enjoying a revival, all of which indicates feverish activity among the forces of darkness. The world is getting ready for the great signs and lying wonders emanating from false Christs and fake prophets, which the tribulation period will have.

PERSONAL SIGNS

As the time of the saint's departure from the world of sin and sobs is at hand, there are several qualities he must exhibit. The saint, himself, will have an inward feeling regarding the nearness of his Lord's return. A strange yet irresistible intuition will be his that Christ is at hand.

> In my heart I have the witness
> That His coming draweth nigh.

It is this fact that accounts for the most unusual interest of the Lord's people in prophetic themes and the reason for their marked detachment from worldly pleasures and a sweeter attachment to Jesus. It is reported of the late General William Booth, founder of the Salvation Army, that in his last days he lost his eyesight completely. On one occasion his daughter, Evangeline, was with him and beholding a most glorious sunset, she appealed to her father to try, if possible, to see something of the glory that was charging her soul. She finally said, "Father, you cannot see the sunset." "No," said the great old general, "but I shall see sunrise." That is the great anchorage for those who are nearing the change of worlds.

1. STEADFASTNESS

The New Testament is insistent in its call to steadfastness as the saint's translation is imminent. He must hold fast to what he has: an infallible Bible; the deity and efficacious death and glorious resurrection of Christ; and integrity of life. We are told to *"stand fast, and hold the traditions which ye have been taught"* (2 Thessalonians 2:15). We are to be diligent lest we fall from our own steadfastness. (See 2 Peter 3:17; Revelation 3:11.) Alas, too many drift! They have no moorings. Doubts are believed, and beliefs are doubted. Lacking deep convictions, they are destitute of courage and purpose.

2. PERSECUTION

Christians are not to be surprised at the fiery ordeal they are being called upon to endure. As the earth becomes riper for judgment, all who live godly in Christ Jesus must suffer persecution. (See 2 Timothy 3:12–13.) They have the promise, however, that suffering for Christ they will also reign with Him. (See 2 Timothy 2:12.) The Lord has not promised His followers immunity from the hard pressure of the adverse circumstances of their own age. The offense of the cross has never ceased. Christians must expect to follow their master in being lightly esteemed if they desire to share in the splendor of His triumph and reign. (See Romans 8:17.) The world, it may be said, does not persecute the professing church. It has been converted to the world, and the world will not persecute its own. But let her return to the Lord and adopt apostolic methods in the exercise of her ministry, and the sore trials of the early church will reappear.

3. DILIGENCE

All who love Christ's appearing will see to it that they are not so heavenly minded as to be of no earthly use. They will not be guilty of stargazing and falling in the mud. Faithfulness in every calling will be a mark of their preparedness. There will be obedience to the Lord's command to *"occupy* [do business] *till I come"* (Luke 19:13). Whether one labors in office, factory, business, home, or church, the very best will be given to one's responsibilities. Conscious that the judgment seat is at hand, where "every man's work is to be tried by fire, of what sort it is," the child of God will strive to be wholehearted, loyal, and true. Dr. J. H. Jowett's comment on Matthew 13:45 is most appropriate:

> If the citizen of the Kingdom of God can be suggestively compared to a merchantman, there must be something about him exceedingly business-like and enterprising.… I am to be as business-like in my religious as in my commercial life.… Men, somehow or other, drop their business instincts when they go about their Father's business. Now this parable is an appeal to men to bring into religion the

same wideawake business capabilities which they exercise in the affairs of the world.[32]

4. HOLINESS

The apostle John emphasizes the sanctifying effect of the second advent. *"Every man that hath this hope in him purifieth himself, even as [Christ] is pure"* (1 John 3:3). We cannot live careless, indifferent lives if we truly believe in Christ's return. Every part of life will be continually adjusted to such a wonderful truth and event. "With such a blessed hope in view, we would more holy be." Here, then, is one way by which we can solve our personal problems. If we have any doubt about anything we countenance, let us ask ourselves the question, "Would I like Jesus to come and find me doing this?" Thus, quickly we can determine its rightness or otherwise. We will not be ashamed at His coming if we go nowhere where we would not go when Jesus comes nor say nothing we would not say when Jesus comes. Beloved, can we say we are ready to meet the Lord? Have we a clear sky, a clean heart, and a consistent witness? As the close of this day may find us in the air with our blessed Lord, will it not be best for us to pause, here and now, and seek the cleansing of the blood for all that would cause us to hang our head with shame at His arrival?

---

32. Dr. J. H. Jowett, *Thirsting for the Springs* (London: H. R. Allenson, 1902), 152–153.

ABOUT THE AUTHOR

When Dr. Herbert Lockyer (1886–1984) was first deciding on a career, he considered becoming an actor. Tall and well-spoken, he seemed a natural for the theater. But the Lord had something better in mind. Instead of the stage, God called Herbert to the pulpit, where, as a pastor, a Bible teacher, and the author of more than fifty books, he touched the hearts and lives of millions of people.

Dr. Lockyer held pastorates in Scotland and England for twenty-five years. As pastor of Leeds Road Baptist Church in Bradford, England, he became a leader in the Keswick Higher Life Movement, which emphasized the significance of living in the fullness of the Holy Spirit. This led to an invitation to speak at the Moody Bible Institute's fiftieth anniversary in 1936. His warm reception at that event led to his ministry in the United States. He received honorary degrees from both the Northwestern Evangelical Seminary and the International Academy in London.

In 1955, he returned to England, where he lived for many years. He then returned to the United States, where he spent the final years of his life in Colorado Springs, Colorado, with his son, the Rev. Herbert Lockyer Jr., a Presbyterian minister who eventually became his editor.

www.ingramcontent.com/pod-product-compliance
Lightning Source LLC
LaVergne TN
LVHW051506070426
835507LV00022B/2951